Billionair
Min...

1/25/20

THE POWER OF MY STORY

*Embracing Struggle To
Unlock Full Potentials*

We are Diamonds

We are Eagles

We are Lions

PATRICE L. DELEVOE JR.

We are Royal

We are Students of Life

Library of Congress Control Number: 2019916123

ISBN: 9781710056464

2020 Visions

Overflow   Peace   Faith

Increase   Love   Hope

THE POWER OF MY STORY

Wealth

To my 3 friends ☺ ,(Micah, Aaron, Sandy)

Thanks for your support alongside this phenomenal journey, keep becoming the best version of yourself and make the world a better place. We have come along ways and have a long ways to go. Please share this book with anyone it can inspire, motivate, or save. You are destined for greatness. May God continue to overflow your cup with peace, love, abundance and generational wealth. God Bless you,

Audible

678-883-6071
Text when you are logged in

Delevoep @yahoo.com

Dlobby 1102

CONTENTS

PREFACE

I'VE BEEN TOLD I need to write a book for an extended period of time now. Being completely honest, I have been procrastinating due to fears, doubts, and uncertainty. Fears enter when I think about being vulnerable to the world. When this book releases these words will stick forever. Many individuals believe I should write a book based on parts of my story, aiming to learn more about my philosophies, or a way to support me on the journey to become a millionaire by 25.

I never knew how I would start at the book. However, I've been listening to Grant Cardone and he said he just starts without thinking about the mistakes or grammatical errors so I'm going to give it a shot. I was at the 3rd annual 10x conference and Grant told us he wrote a book in 7 days. This was unbelievable. I am a firm believer that if one person can do it, another person can. This leads me to put my money where my mouth is.

I would like to start this book giving gratitude to everyone that has motivated, inspired or supported me along this phenomenal journey. I've been through many trials and tribulations. As a youth, I realized life comes with setbacks. However, it's not about how many times you get knocked down but how many times you can get back up without staying down. Life is not meant to be fair, but it's meant to be lived to its full potential.

This book will include sessions with my therapist resurfacing life challenges, battles and obstacles I've faced in my life. It will include great accomplishments as I embrace struggles, challenges and take you on my journey. It will also include information from numerous sources on transformation, personal growth and self-development, financial literacy, health, spiritually and valuable life lessons. The book is real. My life is not perfect, my family is not perfect, my friends are not perfect BUT this book will embrace our imperfections and celebrate the successes of great accomplishments, victories, and triumph. Thanks for the positive reviews.

The mission of this book is to help everyone unlock their full potential. This book is meant to help others get pass their fears, doubts, and adversities. This book will help other embrace changes, challenges, and commitments. This book will inspire others to chase their dreams and understand success is possible. This book will inspire others to take risk instead of settling. This book will help other appreciate the life they have without taking everything for granted. This book will help inspire the leaders in the community to set better examples for the youth. This book will change the lives of millions. This book will help individuals own their stories. This book will break generational curses. This book will make others think twice before judging someone. This book will inspire individuals to examine themselves. This book will help shine light on mental health issues in the African American community. This book will help Millionaires Mindset Academy (MMA) grow into one of the most positive and impactful community organizations in the world. This book will lead by example. My story can inspire others to live life with purpose on purpose. I challenge anyone reading this book to take time to reflect over his or her life story, embrace it and share it with the world. Be inspired, to inspire.

ACKNOWLEDGEMENTS

To my ancestors for enduring unbelievable hardships, accomplishing phenomenons, and setting the bar for future generations to build upon. My mind, body and spirit align to live a purposeful life. I devote my life to inspire others as you have inspired me. I strongly believe it is my responsibility to continue the missions of slaves, great leaders, advocates, philosophers, royal families, and ancient civilizations. I quote Muata Ashby, from Ancient Egyptian Proverb, "O people of the earth, men and women born and made of the elements, but with the spirit of the Divine within you, rise from your sleep of ignorance! Be sober and thoughtful. Realize that your home is not on the earth but in the Light. Why have you delivered yourselves unto death, having power to partake of immortality?" Thank you for helping me travel towards the light on this journey to fulfill my personal legend.

To my grandparents for birthing my parents. Although, I never physically meet my grandfathers, I know they were great men. I only heard great things about both of them. I know they were leaders, innovators and loved their families. I know they made sacrifices to make sure our families established solid foundations to build upon. I aspire to be great like both of them. Thanks for setting a great example and keeping excellent standards. Thanks to my grandmothers for being loving, GOD fearing and keeping our families together. Thanks for being strong, confident and upholding the standards of traditional marriage. Watching your examples helps me keep faith on the journey to pursuing marriage and a lifelong partner. Thanks for leading by example and standing firm on your beliefs. I'm very fortunate and grateful to be a part of our family.

To my parents for molding me to be the best man I could possibly be despite any challenges or hardships. I went through several stages throughout my growth. Thank you for taking time out to converse, hold me accountable and making necessary sacrifices for me to achieve great heights of success at a young age. The morals, principles, values and codes empower me every day to be the best version of myself. It has always been my goal to uphold the family name to an excellent standard, embody our core values and share the love I received to the world. I couldn't have asked for a better set of parents. Thanks for bringing me into our royal families and upholding great standards, ethics, morals and wealthy values. I'm confident this book, accomplishments and positive impacts will serve as small tokens of appreciation.

To my aunties for supporting, providing and being compassionate. You are true Queens. Thanks for supporting me during school functions, business endeavors, birthdays and any other time. Thanks for keeping me on the right track, having high expectations and speaking life over me. Thank you for understanding me on my growth, comforting my mother, and keeping GOD's love present in our family. Thank you for looking over my cousins and keeping them on the right track. Thank you for every Sunday meal, holiday celebration and just because of family moments. I love and value each and every one of you. I'm grateful for all the sacrifices, talks and hugs.

To my uncles for being leaders, businessman, and serving the military. You are amazing men because you set the bar in any area I could pursue in life. I adapt many ethics codes, religious beliefs, and principles from your doctrines. Thank you for protecting our family. Thank you for all the gifts, wisdom, knowledge and understanding through my journey to become a man. Thank you for believing in me and pushing me away from the street life. Thank you for giving me enough room to grow as a man but guiding me with your stories. Thank you for showing me how to be a gentleman with class, style, integrity, and honor. We have been blessed as a family to still be here with each other and I aim to show you appreciation before we depart from one another.

To my brothers for setting great examples and holding me accountable for my actions. Thank you for allowing me to see, hear and experience early adulthood without filters. In reflection, I thank you for trying your best in a neighborhood filled with many influences, mother working countless hours, and little guidance outside of the house. Learning from each positive or negative experience, I was able to make decisions that stuck with me for a lifetime. Thanks for being on call, willing to ride through any situation, and holding me down. Thank you for toughening me up, helping me identify respect, and teaching me about females. Thank you for helping me understand the code and showing me the difference between real and fake at a young age. Thank you for paving the way for me to accomplish greatness, showing me the way and providing opportunity on the phenomenal journey.

To my sisters for showing compassion and pushing me to be a great leader. As a young man, I've always aim to uphold myself to the highest standards. Thanks for showing me simple things about a woman and helping me understand things from a different perspective. Thanks for having the awkward conversations I wouldn't have with my mother or older aunties. Thanks for giving me a place to stay when I needed a mental break or escape from my created chaos. Thanks for helping me develop a great character and stay focused on my education. I'm grateful and will forever remember each moment, sacrifice, and simple thing.

To my children, grandchildren and future generations for coming to me in dreams, visions and spirit. You are not born in this physical world yet. Thank you for giving me the drive to continue this journey. I choose the path less traveled. This path may leave some bruises, tears and scrapes but I'm paving the way for you. I accept the obligation to grant each and every one of you a fulfilling life with many great possibilities. Thank you being the best version of yourself every day. Thank you for showing the world what winners are made of. Thank you for showing the world unconditional love. Thank you for having integrity, strength, and wisdom. Thank you for accepting the terms and conditions to continue this family legacy.

To my cousins for being so original, dope and leading by example. Our accomplishments, ambitions, and relentlessness show we have greatness within our bloodline. Thanks for believing in me.

Thanks for sticking up for me. Thanks for supporting my dreams. Thanks for being a great family member. Thanks for motivating me in action. Thanks for being there through all the tough times. Thanks for protecting me and showing me lessons about life. Thanks for providing a blueprint and trusting me. Thank you for showing me that there are consequences behind every choice or action. Thanks for helping me change my life. Thanks for helping me embrace life.

To my nephews for becoming Kings. Continue to set the bar high and strive to be the best version of yourself. Remember to always lead by example. You have greatness within you, and you will accomplish many phenomenal things in life. GOD has blessed you with countless opportunities and I look forward to seeing you take advantage of them. Let this book serve as a reminder that times will get challenging, battles will arise, but GOD will never leave nor forsake you. Become the best man you could possibly become. We're here to assist you along the way.

To my many nieces for becoming Queens. I'm working in a smart way to establish more foundations for our families. Do not settle or lower your expectations in life. Remain pure in all ways of your life. Remember, you can always call on us and GOD. I've watched each and every one of you grow into young princesses. Success will continue to come piece by piece. Fulfillment will come piece by piece. Life will manifest into what you want it to be piece by piece. Remain patience, loving, kind, and compassionate. Keep your smiles wide, glows bright, and mind sharp. The road ahead is going to be worth it.

To my business partners for listening to my insane business ideas, generating enough courage to build with me, and trusting the process throughout the business ups and downs. I will always remember the times we stayed up late planning, days we shared aiming to reach goals, and priceless moments. Thanks for believing in the visions and missions of the companies. If I have not learned anything, I've definitely learned how to loosen up and have a little fun while building. Creative masterminding is essential to long term growth. Thanks for being great business partners all around. May we continue to build, grow and develop in the world's greatest creators and innovators.

To my mentors for being the best version of yourself and showing me, anything is possible if you have the right mindset. Thank you for taking time out of your busy schedules to write book, record videos, embrace change and lead by example. Being able to see someone that has faced the same battles, adversities, and challenges to succeed is inspiring. Often as an entrepreneur, it is difficult to relate to others but having caring mentors really help. Thanks for pouring into me and helping me embrace the concept of service to mankind.

To my future millionaires' and billionaires' mentees for being coachable and committed to the process. Thank you for accepting me as a leader as you grow and develop into the best version of yourself. I aim to share as much love, wisdom, knowledge, and understanding as possible on your journey. I advise you to continue to strive for greatness and chase your dreams without doubt. The road ahead has long term benefits. Thanks for allowing me to be a vessel to you. Keep your winner mindset and stay positive.

To my supporters for holding me to an excellent standard and continuously guiding me in business and life. There have been times when I was lost, confused and stuck in the midst of depression. The uplifting messages, expectations of greatness, financial support, and even smiles has helped me get through the toughest challenges. Knowing each and every one of you are watching help keep me focused on the end result. I can and will not let you down. Thanks for letting me know I inspire, motivate, and grant hope. Reading the messages gives me hope and affirms I am not making sacrifices in vain.

To my significant other for trusting the process as we build a strong union. I know it's not easy, fast paced or simple beings committed to a growing entrepreneur. Thank you for cheering me on and supporting me through my transitions. Thank you for investing time and energy into my dreams while pursuing yours. Thank you for helping me pick up the broken pieces and put them back together to love you. I appreciate everything you have done, and each sacrifice made to help me stay at the top of my game.

To my teachers for being patient with me and guided me in my growth. Thanks for each time you separated me from distractions, took extra time out to help me understand concepts, or pushed me to achieve greatness in your class. Thanks for not lowering your standards and setting the bar. I've enjoyed stepping up to each challenge even if I did not completely understand while in your class. I appreciated every talk before and after class. Thanks for seeing the best in me.

To the positive OGs for blessing me with knowledge, wisdom, love and understanding. Thanks for keeping me on my pivot. As a youth, it's easy to get lost in the streets. Thanks for helping me learn from your life stories. Thanks for showing me different routes. Thanks for all the positive advice. Thanks for treating me like family and adapting me. There are many things I did not experience or attempt following your leadership.

To the negative OGs for showing me what they could. Thanks for allowing me to get burnt by fire. Life comes with its fair share of individuals. I hope each and every one of you learn from mistakes. Life is valuable and everyone deserves a chance to live it to the fullest. Get out of your comfort zone and make an attempt to live differently. Try something positive and build great habits.

To the people who doubted me for motivating me to help you believe in yourself. Thank for motivating me to beat the odds without becoming a statistic. Thanks for pointing out my weaknesses and flaws so I can improve upon them. Thanks for putting fuel on the burning fire deep inside of my soul. I once heard a song that states, "If you don't have any haters you are not popping." So, I would like to give you a warm thanks for inspiring me to pop and be the best version of myself daily. I send positive vibrations and pray for your healing.

GOD bless you each and every one of you. May your life be filled with an abundance of wealth, endless joy, everlasting happiness, inner peace, infinite prosperity, pure love, GOD's wisdom, universal knowledge, and conscious understanding.

INTRODUCTION

I MAGINE A FOUR-YEAR-OLD BOY who loses his innocence through-out his childhood to trusted family members and older public housing friends. Visualize growing up in a cold world through his tainted lens. Picture seven-year-old thoughts as his mother and fathers undergo a life changing divorce. Or a chubby fat middle school teen who lacks confidence due to man boobs, misunder-stood dark skin, unpopular distinctive facial features, predominantly female name and a high-pitched voice. Think about the odds stacked against African-American adolescents growing up in poverty from a single parent home. Imagine losing family members to death, incar-ceration, or common neighborhood struggles. Can one personally grow and self-develop into positive example, become a courageous leader, or self-made multimillionaire under these conditions?

I've heard so many stories of individuals who became overnight successes. The term "overnight success" is a loosely used term to describe someone who achieves massive levels of success within the blink of an eye. After examining their stories, I recognized the success came from a relentless effort to achieve their goals. The success came from dedication, drive, and determination. The suc-cess was a result of hard work, strategy, and preparation. These individuals just so happened to be prepared when opportunity presented itself. However, I discovered many of these individual's inspirational success story are birthed from pain, traumas, grievances, abuse, homelessness, abandonment, and so forth. They were all diamonds in the rough.

As a diamond in the rough, I transformed into an "overnight success". This intense process was not a simple walk in the park. The "overnight success" came from many nights of depression, anxiety, shame, guilt, and many other negative emotions. I was tired of feeling sorry for myself. I was tired of blaming my environment. I was tired of blaming the system. I was tired of losing my identity. I was fed up. The "overnight success" came from countless nights of grind, sacrifice, prayers, fasts, books, podcasts, plans, and countless enrichment tools. I am committed. I am determined. I am driven. I am working. I am learning. I am becoming the best version of myself. I am embracing my struggles. I am unlocking my full potential.

It's September 11th and I am over 30,000 feet in the air traveling first class from Washington, D.C to Pensacola, Florida. Pensacola International Airport is almost three hours away from my final destination. I missed my connecting flight to Tallahassee, Florida due to a delay. By the Grace of GOD, this special flight was delayed for two hours. It's the last flight available heading in the direction of the 1% Event in New Orleans, LA. My seatmate on the previous flight name was Tamarra J. Yes, it's pronounced similar to Tomorrow!!! I was working on the book, told her about my plans for tomorrow and the possibilities of missing my connector flight. When we landed, she told me to make every second count. I ran from the flight, took a shuttle bus from one side of the airport to the other, and arrived at my original connector flight terminal. I discovered my Tallahassee flight left on-time. After running terminal to terminal seeking other options, a voice told me to go to the customer service desk. I began to express the importance of the trip, my plans and so forth. The sweet elderly lady at the desk stopped me in my rant to tell me about this special flight. She told me to hurry because I could not risk missing it. I was the last passenger to board within seconds of departure.

I'm grateful my sister, Shakeria Dillard, Founder and CEO of Cleaning with Care, is prepared to attend this event with me. She will be able to pick me up from the airport when I land. We're excited to meet Eric Thomas and his Associates. After much anticipation, we will finally hear them pour knowledge, wisdom, and understanding into us live and in person. Reflecting over the past couple weeks on tour, I've attended a private Yacht Party in Hollywood, Florida with marketing gurus, successful entrepreneurs, and affluent individuals. I've jogged throughout Miami Brickell Key recording inspirational, motivational, and exercise videos. I've served my sister Angel Olofin, Founder of Boss Women International & A Taste of Angel, as she builds phenomenal relationships as a celebrity chef for Quality Control Music Group. I've served and prayed for ambitious homeless individuals in Atlanta, GA. I've served followers, mentees, and business partners via emails, phone calls, and inspirational posts. I've been waking up in 5-star hotels with breathtaking views to find additional sources of inspiration to keep writing this phenomenal story. I'm blessed to discover resources, unlock "hidden" potentials, and start a 30 days lifestyle transformation with Arbonne. I'm connected with my Wilcoxson, Smith, Delevoe, Havana, and extended family. I love each and every one of you so much. I'm communicating with friends, associates and loved one to keep them uplifted, supported and inspired. I'm preparing for our 40th Celebration of Reverend Samuel Delevoe Day. I'm back on track for graduation, passing all of my online educational courses, and educating others. I'm leading by example. I'm showing others it's possible to take control of your life. I'm showing others it's possible to live your dreams. My mind, body, and soul are all in alignment. I'm living my dreams, prayers, and manifestations.

Here's a GEM: *Sometimes you are delayed not denied.* I was listening to a YouTube motivational video featuring Les Brown. He was instructing listeners to expect good things to happen to them. I received the message. I decided to say, "Phenomenal things will happen." Our thoughts become things. Our language shapes our reality. Reflecting back, I recognized I had to embrace struggles to unlock my full potential. I did not have everything figured out when I began this journey. I'm similar to Santiago, a 'young shepherd' boy, from the book of The Alchemist pursuing his personal legend with the universe as a guide. Great omens have been appearing in the form of phenomenal individuals, synchronicity, and aligned opportunities. I stopped forcing things in my life. I learned how to be in peace and harmony with the universe. Everything I was looking for was already inside of me. I found my strength. It was stored in my struggles. It was stored in my testimonies. It was stored potential.

The potential has been waiting on me to unlock it. My own personal treasure. I locked away so many thoughts, memories, and parts of my life. I sweep so much "dirt" under the rug and tossed bags of "garbage" to the back of the closet. I was focused on being perfect in an imperfect world. This created a sense of confusion. I lost parts of my drive. I lost sight of what got me so far. I lost my own identity. A wise man once said, one-man trash is another man's treasure. It just so happens that I am the same man with an enhanced mindset. The "dirt" and "garbage" were my own personal treasures. Generational struggles caused intense pressure and heat beyond the capacity of articulation. My mindset before failing would not allow me to see full value. My mindset before Millionaires Mindset Academy would not allow me to see full value. My mindset before my therapist sessions would not allow me to see full value. My mindset before myself examination would not allow me to see full value. My mindset before aligning my mind, body, and soul would not allow me to see full value.

I was not embracing my struggles. I was running from them. I did not want to carry the responsibility of being Patrice L. Delevoe Jr. I did not want to become a public speaker. I did not want to become a minster. I did not want to embrace my struggles because I didn't want to acknowledge my own flaws. I did not want to surrender to the will of GOD. I came to a conclusion. It was not about my wants. It's about my purpose. I was sent here for a purpose. To discover my purpose, I had to be less of me and more of GOD. My therapist manuscripts are artifacts that will serve as an introduction to beginning chapters. I examined my thoughts, thoroughly read and analyzed them. My enhanced mindset adjusted my focus. I cut out the negative thinking. My enhanced mindset beautifully polished my struggles and opened my eyes. My enhanced mindset saw diamonds instead of "dirt" and "garbage". Here's a truthful memoir and powerful transformation story. It starts with my first emergency session with my therapist.

FIRST EMERGENCY SESSION
WITH MY THERAPIST

July 29, 2017
3:27am

MY STORY BEGINS WITH the birth of my mother, Cheryl Deloris Wilcoxson Delevoe. She was raised in Havana, FL, a small rural town in Gadsden County. She is the daughter of Odessa Wilcoxson (Grandmother) and Raymond Wilcoxson (Grandfather).

------- *RESTART* -------

My Grandmother and Grandfather on my Mom's side were Indians.

My Great Grandfather on my father's side of the family was a former plantation worker, who later migrated from the Bahamas to Miami, FL, and began working as a carpenter. After he passed, his son (my Grandfather) relocated to the Broward area (Hollywood, Ft. Lauderdale, Dania, Florida).

He created a community subdivision that began to empower the community and help it excel. He was assassinated by someone he was aiming to help. My Grandmother was there. She was shot also. She held him and loved on him as he bled out and took his last breath. At a young age, my Dad witnessed his parents get shot.

My Grandmother never remarried. I've never seen her with another man. She is the Bishop of On This Rock Ministries. My Uncle is the Pastor. My Father is the ministry of music. He plays several instruments including the drums, piano, and sings.

My Mother is the happiest, uplifting, loving, caring, and sweet individual. However, she is also known for standing her ground if you mess with her in the wrong way, but you will respect her and she will love you. Knowing her affords an opportunity to have one of the longest, best relationships you could ever have. She is going to be real with you, so be real with her. If I advise people on how to be, I would tell them to be like my Mom—do the right thing and treat people how you want to be treated.

She has 11 brothers and sisters of Havana, FL. I have four Aunties on my mother's side of the family. One was a manager at Family Dollar, one is a manager over an apartment complex Riverside Apartments, one lives up north, and one reminds me of my mother. Three aunts are married with happy families. One of my aunt's significant other passed, Long Live Uncle Dudley. Our family has always valued family, because we were all we ever had. We had each other, and we didn't really have too many friends, and the friends that we did and do are considered family as well—"family friends".

That's one difference I noticed about a country way of living and a city way of living—you can't find too many "family-friends". In the country you find a lot of "family friends" because you go to each other's family's house and you get to know each other's families. In the city, there is usually so many people there and so many things can happen—it can be dangerous, so the way that people interact is different. Even though the country can be dangerous too (i.e. getting into fights or getting lost on back roads) its general culture is centered on genuine hospitality, togetherness, and family. For example, if you go to anyone's house in the country and someone has cooked, you can be sure that you will be fed, and not only fed but you will eat good, meaning, when someone prepares your plate of food it will have enough food on it to actually cover two plates and you'll be stuffed. In the country, we are big cooks and heavy handed.

------ *BREAK* ------

I tried to go to Havana Elementary School. I grew up in Havana Riverside, apt. 149R. The apartments were known as "the projects on the hill". I remember walking in the house after school and I would always smell some food. Throughout my childhood my weight would fluctuate. I attribute that to being physically active. I would play sports and run outside all day, but I would also say it was due to depression. Depression has always been a common factor in my life, even during childhood. It's just something that has always been there. I define depression as an experience of repetitive bouts of sadness rooted in circumstances and events that have happened to me in my life. I believe this eventually leads to a chemical imbalance in the brain that induces "random sadness", even when my current life circumstances are ideal. I am not sure how long this process takes, but I wonder how long it takes for this chemical change to happen in the brain.

I also think I have post-traumatic stress disorder from my cousin passing and other things that have happened.

----- BREAK -----

I went to Gadsden Elementary Magnet School. It was originally named Midway Magnet because it was initially located in Midway, FL, in the middle of nowhere. I went there for kindergarten. Previously, I went to pre-k at Havana Elementary School. Because I was recognized as being smart and gifted, the faculty and staff recommended that I go to Midway Magnet. From there my Mother put me in private school at Midway Magnet. I enjoyed going there.

Growing up I had difficulties pronouncing certain letters and sounds, like my r, s, and I, so I was enrolled into a speech class. I was picked on 2-3 times every week for my speech impediment. I had a really good friend named Greg, who was in the class with me. He had difficulties with stuttering. I also had a friend name Regan, she was a good friend to me. She was also in the class. I had so many good friends at Midway Magnet. We were the schools' very first class of student and we set the bar. It became an A school known for excellence. We had the best of the best teachers working with us. I was in the gifted program. The teachers there always made sure we were exposed to a variety of subjects and experiences, introducing us to art and cultures from all over the world. We would take field trips and partake in hands on learning during "special area classes". Special area was a class that allowed us to participate in chorus and learn about playing various instruments such as the violin.

When I went to 3rd grade they moved us from Midway to Gadsden Elementary Magnet School in Quincy, FL.

------ BREAK ------

See the thing is… back in my brother's generation. Quincy and Havana had a history of rivalry. When I started 3rd grade at Gadsden Elementary Magnet school, I brought that mentality into the school because that's all I knew, so I didn't like the kids from Quincy nor did I associate myself with them. But the longer I was there I became cool with the kids there. It was there that I met Landus Anderson, one of the best basketball players of his time and my first best friend. I also met Jakari Dupont…we were great friends. We were in the Links Beautillion program together.

----BREAK -----

My principle nominated me to participate in this program after getting in trouble at school one day. I recall getting in trouble for talking back or being loud. I was this way because I knew I was not dumb, and I refused to be talked to and treated as such.

------BREAK------

The teachers at Godby High School really treated us like a family.

-----BREAK------

I've always had great encounters with people unless we were in the streets.

-------BREAK-------

I've been through a lot but I'm a great person… I will inspire and motivate the world….

-------BREAK-------

I can... I will… I must

FALLS ASLEEP

Ends first EMERGENCY therapy session

1

ENRICHED FOUNDATION

A WISE MAN ONCE TOLD me, "Life is 10% what happens to you and 90% how you react to it." Over the past 24 years, I've been embracing the process of transformation to become the best version of myself. The best version of myself is not easily moved by external forces, but internally fulfilled. The best version of myself has mastered personal growth and self-development, financial literacy, spiritually, health, peace and harmony, and education. The best version of myself is a phenomenon. Committing to this process has not been an easy task due to learned behaviors in my childhood, adolescence, and young adulthood. Currently, I'm having a hard time opening up and pouring out my life story into this book. I'm debating if putting out my personal life story is the right thing to do. In this thought, I received a precious GEM: *"You went through trials and tribulation to help inspire others so embrace your story."* However, there's a fear of the unknown. Don't worry, I will push pass all fears to enlighten you. Throughout this book, I will mentally open up describing stories, philosophies, and additional valuable information. My therapy sessions will lead into some chapters. The purpose of this book is to make a positive impact and change lives. I know there are kids, students and adults purchasing this book as a source of inspiration. I will not allow my doubts or fears to hold this book back from being a true source. So, here's my reaction to the 10%.

I believe a concrete; deep foundation is the most important part of building anything successful. The Burj Khalifa skyscraper, tallest building in the world, is a world-class destination and the magnificent centerpiece of Downtown Dubai, Dubai's new urban masterpiece. The tower foundations consist of a solid, 3.7-meter (12.1-foot) thick pile supported raft poured utilizing 12,500 cubic meters of C50 cube strength self-consolidating concrete. Without the tower foundations, Burj Khalifa skyscraper, the tallest building in the world would have collapsed upon building. My life concrete foundation has been poured with numerous experiences, countless circumstances, inspirational trauma and supported by persistent personal growth and self-development, divine intervention, loving family, friends, and supporters.

Growing up in Havana, Florida has been a pleasant experience. Havana is a small town in Gadsden County, Florida. It's a small suburb of Tallahassee, Florida. The population is under 1,800. Growing up in a small town has pros and cons. Here's some examples, everyone seems to know each other, a deep appreciation for family, and community involvement. On the other hand, rumors spread like wildfire, community gossip is common, and lack of immediate resources. The experience has deeply rooted and appreciated small village cultural values. At the age of seven, I watch my household foundation fall without much understanding.

In 2001, I watch my mother and father get a divorce. Due to my lack of understating, I begin to develop a heightened sense of anger and wild burst of anger. Initially, I would take my anger out on anyone who looked at me wrong or triggered my emotions. I aimed to eliminate anger by staying isolated from others or staying busy working on projects. I locked myself in the room doing educational work or practicing being an engineer with hot wheels or I would play football to release the energy on the field. We lived in R-149 in Riverside apartments located in Havana, Florida. Informally known as the new projects on the hill. Our community came with its fair share of positive OGS, hustlers, individuals affected by life circumstances and a wide range of successful business owners. I've grown to have an optimistic look on life instead of focusing on what we "lacked" as a community. We look out for each other. We protect each other. It's similar to a village. Many refer to Havana as Lil Haiti.

We have two traffic lights intersections, a few restaurants, some cool country folk, and a few back roads. We didn't have the best educational systems, highest proven incomes, or wide range of city resources. Conversely, we did have a loving community where everyone knows everyone. We have a strong town pride. We learn how to stick together and protect each other at an early age. This could be a good thing or a bad thing. I will not go into details or disclose but if you come from a small town, I'm sure you have the capacity to understand.

Growing up, I was the youngest of three brothers. Being the youngest automatically placed an enormous amount of pressure on me because I had vivid examples. Failure was not an option. Both of my brothers are older than me, so I grew up being a part of two older generations before my generation began to "jump off the porch". The term "jump off the porch" means you leave from around supervision to experience things in life outside of your normal activity. My first time seeing and experiencing numerous things were in the presence of my brothers or their associates. Although they aimed to shelter and protect me, I still got exposed to many things at a young age.

In 2003, Havana Northside High School of Havana, Florida and James A Shanks High School of Quincy, Florida merged to form East Gadsden High School. The cities were rivals. I remember one night we went to a football game at East Gadsden High School. Upon leaving a brawl started between my brother's associates and a group from Quincy. One fight, all fight. I remember helping an associate fight a guy from the opposing side. We jumped in the car and left before the police came to arrest anyone. Fighting became a learned behavior. I already had built up anger and resentment from my mother and father divorce.

After the divorce, life transformed without me noticing. I would spend summers and vacations in Fort Lauderdale, Florida but I never thought much of it. Everyone still seemed joyful with bright smiles, so I didn't recognize any immediate damage. African-America families are great at suppressing pain, ignoring conversations, and smiling despite adversity. I received the best of both worlds. The country life with my mother's side of the family. The city life with my dad's side of the family.

My first time flying in a plane was a flight from Tallahassee, Florida to Fort Lauderdale, Florida. My grandmother Dr. Delevoe and Dad wanted me to arrive as soon as possible because our family was preparing a Christian conference. This was one of the biggest Christian Conferences in South Florida. I remember seeing my grandmother appear on television informing the viewers about the upcoming event. Preparing to come down, I was not old enough to catch a bus by myself. They booked me a flight through Delta Airlines. The flight was a great experience. I remember the beautiful flight attendant chauffeured me around. They gave me a VIP treatment. I got an up-close tour of the cockpit. The experience sparked a dream to become a pilot. Although I'm not currently pursuing a dream of becoming a pilot yet, I jumped off the porch as an entrepreneur, servant, and leader.

My Grandmother Dr. Delevoe, Uncle Sam, Dad, Brother ET and I would pray every morning. Often, we would pray and worship GOD for hours at a time. The Holy spirit would enter and spread throughout each one of us. I was young but I still remember some of my prayers. Here's a GEM: *Being grounded in the word and trusting the Holy spirit has really helped me get through tough situations and prosper in life.*

As a member of On This Rock I'll Build My Church Ministry, & South Florida Leaders of Tomorrow, Inc., I was exposed to meeting different business owners, activist, Christian entertainers, and supporters at a young age. I remember running business to business and around neighborhoods smiling saying, "Hi, I'm from On This Rock Ministries will you support our church by giving a donation please?" This was a new experience for me, but I was excited to provide community service while earning money.

Throughout this process, I saw different sides in the communities. I saw drug addicts, drug dealers, even hood fights. I saw business owners, street hustlers, and block celebrations. We explored Pompano, Deerfield, Sunrise, Hollywood, and many other locations in South Florida. Once we were raising money, my friend and I saw a table with guys playing dominos, so I said, "Let's go ask them...." I was familiar with the environment because it was similar to back home in our community cookouts. One of the OGs, as we would call them back home, reached into his pocket pulled out a stack of money and gave up $100 each. He motivated us and told us to keep doing great things in the community. Our faces lit up as we ran back to the car and explained to my grandmother Dr. Delevoe.

She is the Bishop of On This Rock Ministry. She parked the car and walked around to meet the group. I was nervous at first. I thought I was going to have to go to war about my Grandmother. She began to pray for all everyone, bless the money and environment. She did not want us to accept the money at first, but he insists. Reflecting, I observed his interaction with his family on the domino table versus his behavior with my grandmother. We were in the heart of the hood, but GOD presence speaks volumes in any environment. The moment always stuck with me as I explore the different neighborhoods. I learned to pray and never felt unsafe even running with buckets of dollars and change.

Although I earned money over the summers, I still didn't make enough money to buy new release Jordan's or high-end designer clothes out the mall. My mother made sure I had everything I needed. Our school dress code consisted of navy blue, white and hunter green collar shirts with khaki shorts or pants. We could only wear black or brown dress shoes. This was perfect because I could repeat uniforms without anyone knowing. I was instructed to take my clothes off as soon as I get home. My mother taught me how to iron around 7 years old. She wanted me to understand responsibility. At times to surprise her, I would iron her clothes for the week. She was always working, providing and gracefully smiling. This was a small token of gratitude to show her I appreciate her.

My mother made sure my brothers, family, loved ones and I had a roof over our heads, clothes on our backs and food to eat daily. She worked overnights and would work doubles sometimes. My middle brother ET and I would cook food to make sure everyone eats. My brother ET worked at restaurants when he was younger. He makes the best wings in the neighborhood. People would ask him to make wings for their parties or our family events. I learned as much as I could from him. He would show me different ways to fry, season, and cut things. My mother and Dad would show me different tips too.

I found a passion for cooking at a young age. The process of cooking is similar to the process of life. You either shop around to get new ingredients or scramble around to make something with the ingredients available. You allow your creativity to kick in. You establish a plan for what you're preparing. You prepare and season food for your guest or personal desires. Allow the food to marinate to deepen the favor. Preheat the cooking equipment. Began the cooking process and pay attention to your pots. As the ingredients come together to manifest the final dish, set out the plates. Fix your plate and top with garnish to enhance the aesthetics. Phenomenal cooking requires discipline, skills, patience, and creativity. Phenomenal individuals display the same traits. I learn the importance of discipline at a young age. I learned the importance of building skills at a young age. I learned the importance of patience at a young age. I learned how to be creative at a young age. I learned responsibility at a young age.

My responsibility as a kid consisted of putting 120% of effort into anything I was required to do. I was required to keep our home clean, get to the bus stop on time and bring home the best grades possible without getting into trouble at school. I completed every task but sometimes my temper would get the best of me. Growing up in an environment full of older brothers and their associates, I learned to be very tough at a young age. I was conditioned to go to war with anybody, big or small. I did not like for anyone to talk to me any type of way. I was taught to earn my respect, but it was not going to be given to me. Once one of my classmates brushed against me because he was upset, and we began to have a brawl in the class. Everybody ran up to me telling me how I did him. Internally, I was not intending to do him any type of way, I just wanted him to respect me the same way I respected him. This happened in one of my favorite teachers' classes, Mr. Johnson. He tried to keep both of us from getting suspended, but the word got out about our fight. This was a common thing even though I did extremely well in my classes.

Throughout grade school, I received much guidance and mentorship. Reflecting back, now I understand the amount of patience my instructors, principals, guidance pour into our relationships. There would be times when my temper would explode, or I would completely shut down mentally. I would even crack a few jokes to get some attention. Somehow, they always found a way to motivate or get me to understand. Sometimes, I could be as simple a threat of calling my mother. My mother would always warn me if I get into any major trouble she would come to class and embarrass me. She told me, "she would whoop my behind in front of the class." She always said, "Wherever you act up, that's where I'm going to get you." Those words stuck with me. Wholeheartedly, I knew she would. So, I learned to be politically correct. I stood up for the things I believed at a young age. I realized my temper issue stemmed from passion. I was passionate about the things I discussed so I felt like I had to prove a point whenever I was misunderstood.

As elementary school proceeded, I began to dominate in education. Instead of me using my physical abilities, I began to use my brain to prove points. I would debate, play chess, math competitions, or Tropicana speeches. Additionally, I began playing football for Havana Wildcats, so I was able to take my anger out on the field. I was skilled playing neighborhood football, but I still had many things to learn aiming to play on a recreational team. After a few late practices, studying the playbook and taking advice from my brother. I was dedicated and became a starting player. I played offense and defense, so I know both sides of the field. I was giving all my energy to football. My big brother, ET, was an All-American football player. He grew up playing football and training with my dad. He was put into the best camps and coached by the best coaches. Miami Dolphins was looking at him in middle school. He motivated me to continue to outwork everybody. I continued to play football and stayed out of trouble throughout the rest of my elementary school years.

Although Gadsden Elementary Magnet School was located in Quincy, I developed some lifelong friendships there. My classmates actually were not that bad, they weren't bad at all. I grew to understand; I adapted the wrong mentality. I was forced to unlearn and relearn. It must have been pretty effective because I would receive 4 and 5 on the FCAT. I would score in the top percentile on state test. I was introduced to a gifted program. My gifted program teacher was from my hometown. I was convinced she had it out for me. I remember getting all the As and a B in gifted class. I was furious. It was the first time I ever would have had all As consecutively. I carried that hurt around for a while. I eventually got over it when I was chosen as Salutatorian. I was faced with a new problem.

This is going to sound crazy. I never had a problem making jokes, fighting, or causing a ruckus. Yet, I was terrified of giving a speech at our graduation. I would think about my anxiety. I could not pronounce the word "extra". I wanted to tell everyone; we were an extraordinary class. Somehow, I found a way to change the word on my speech. I remember my voice cracking and shaking. I rehearse the speech at least 100 times. I could possibly be exaggerating but

I surely doubt it. Anytime, I had to perform or speak my heart would flutter. By the grace of GOD, I got it done. I remember my auntie Margret yelling and my mother. They have always been great supporters. After a few sentences, I was speaking and delivering. I didn't even notice my "speech impediment". Outside of my anxiety attacks, fights, and ego, I was afforded a great foundation of education. I even created some great friends.

Landus Anderson was one of my best friends there. He helped me understand Quincy better. One year it was his birthday and he invited classmates to come visit and stay over. His dad took us around on his motorcycle. Landus and I walked to the park to play basketball. Initially, I thought it was set up, but I was going to fold. It was simply a walk to the park to hang out with other kids. This was a great experience because I never liked Quincy until this experience. Basketball was not my favorite sport. I was talented in Football with dreams of going to the NFL. I think that's almost every kid dream coming from our environment. I know, it was something about being able to be free on the field that gave me additional hope.

My dreams of becoming a pro football player was short lived when I switched schools. On our championship game day, I switched to Florida State University School. I was excited about change, but we actually played them for the championship. Havana Middle School lost by seven points. The score was 0-7, I believe if I was on the team, we would have beat them. This hurt me to my core because I'm loyal. This sacrifice was for the greater good of my educational, personal and economic development. However, My Havana spirit echoed through the hallways and most of the students didn't like me initially. I remember telling my mother, I wanted to wait until the end of the school year, but she explained to me I've been waiting on the waiting list for almost two years. I didn't argue with her. I trust her judgement because I knew she would not tell me anything wrong. Arriving to FSUS, I was amazed at the environment. The school was large, clean and spread out for each stage of grade school. This school help me understand the importance of a positive environment.

During this time period, we experienced many changes. Reflecting back, I watched my mother move us out of the projects to a single-family home down the road. This was an advancement; we didn't have any neighbors connected so we couldn't hear anyone hitting the walls. I wasn't fighting my neighbors and hanging out in the projects became optional. We had our own yard and my mother planted flower trees. In the spring, I remember the roses would bloom beautifully. I would pick some and bring to her to show her love and appreciation. She would put in countless hours to ensure we had everything we needed. In addition to us, she would open the doors to anyone that was going through a hard time. My brother friends, cousins, whoever really. She would always say, "A roof over my head is a roof over many." It was always in her heart to show love to people. We would have cookouts and the entire projects would come to our house. My mother would fix so many plates, she would forget to put her up one. We started noticing we would have to put her up a plate because she would not be focused on herself. This was a different type of love. She tried her best to keep me away from the streets.

I remember one time this older dude stole some money out of her purse. He was around 19, I was only around 14 or 15. He was considered a jit to my brothers, but they knew I didn't mind taking the fade. A fade is a term used in neighborhood to represent a fight or handle a situation. I didn't say anything, but everyone knew the consequences. It's certain things you don't do like you don't steal from nobody's mother in the hood. Everybody in the hood is over protective over their mothers. Most of the dads already gone, so mother is pretty much all we got left in the household. I came home from school one day, my brother told me they saw him again. He came out to his cousin house up in the projects. We snuck out the house and headed up the road. I hopped out the car before my brother could park and headed towards the step. He was upstairs with his cousins. This wasn't like a school fight. In the neighborhood, there's no rules to fighting and nobody is going to break it up unless somebody down and out.

I was not thinking about the circumstances or consequences. I just knew this savage stole from our household. As I thought about it again, I ran up the steps and took off, swung, on him. He stumbled back into a door and the door burst open. I dropped him, got on top of him and started talking to him as I punished him. I remember seeing some blood and heard a gun cock. I heard a voice forcefully say, "Y'all n***** get out the way and back the f*** up". My brothers picked me up and said, "let's slide". I walked out the door and I saw my mother pulling up jumping out the car to grab me. The entire projects were outside trying to see what was going on. We left the old projects and drove to the new projects across the street. My mother began telling me not to ever go to anyone's house to fight. She explained the dangers of it. I could've been killed or injured. I would've been in the wrong regardless of the prior events. She told me she was not worried about the money. I told her; it was the principle of the situation.

All of us was posted outside, when a big crowd cross the road heading from the old projects to the new project. I jumped off the car and was about to square up to run it again. They put me in the house and told me I was not fighting anybody. I already handled it. I sat down in the living room to calm my nerves because I was on whatever. I was gone take it there. However, they wanted to do it. Whenever they wanted to do it. They had a litigation outside. The crowd walked back over to the old projects. The police were not called, no guns were shot, and nobody got seriously injured. I never had any more problems in the neighborhood from the older people. The older homies respected me; his cousins even respected me. They told me they thought he was gone whoop me, but it was messed up what he did. Everybody loves and respect my mother because she always shows love to everybody. It was just a heated day in the neighborhood.

At the age of 15, we moved from our neighborhood to the out-skirts of the town. My mother never really said it but I'm sure she didn't want me to get too caught up in the environment. I remember riding in the car, looking out the window and seeing a sign by a house in the middle of a field. I asked her to stop and I ran around the field. I ran to the back yard to notice a pond of water. We counted

4 bedrooms and 2 bathrooms. This was more than enough space considering my brothers, nieces and nephews.

I always had dreams of moving us out of the neighborhood. I knew I was going to be the biggest football star and a successful businessman. I always said I would be a doctor and a lawyer too. I said I could not just be one. However, my mother did it before I got the chance to be either. She always explained the importance of being a leader, not a follower. As a single parent, I watched her set the bar without little to no assistance. We did not receive food stamps, child support, or any other welfare. I remember hearing others talk about their government assistance, but my dad would have to be put on child support. My mother didn't believe it was necessary or ethical. We made it work. I watched her lead the family as the head of the household.

Although I have a phenomenal mother, growing up without a father directly in the house began to consciously take a toll on me in my adolescence. Growing up into a man there's questions you want to ask someone you trust. Questions you are not going to ask your mother. There are things you can learn from watching him as the head of household. My brothers were still growing and developing into men themselves. My GODfather, Bruce Lovett, died when I was in the 5th grade. I had other male examples and models, but I did not fully trust them to open up about situations outside of the household. I was not about to tell them the things I would do to make money, the risk I take, or the adversities I faced. As far as they were concerned, my grades were great, and I was doing well.

I had a solid group of extended family members. We formed a brotherhood and they became my brothers. Most of us came from broken families, same neighborhood, or faced similar struggles. We could relate to each other. So, we protected, motivated and looked out for each other. I watched my big brothers' brotherhoods, so I was very selective about the type of association, friends, etc. I didn't want to be around anyone that was soft. I didn't want to be around anyone that would fold under pressure. I didn't want to be around anyone that could not hold their own. We had wounds but we were tough, trained to go, and the life of every party. There are many stories I could share with you but that's for another book. Going to other cities to party was a common thing back when we were growing up. I was driving and we would stack up in the Ford Expedition to "hang out". We never looked for trouble but somehow before the party end, we would have to defense ourselves. I remember one time; we were at a party in Quincy and they broke into the truck to steal an amp that connected to the speaker in the back. We were furious and chase them down. We aimed to have a great time without violence but somehow the thing we did not want always attracted itself.

We entered cities collecting generational beefs. Beefs are grudges held by rivals or someone who has a major issue with you. I remember going to a party in Tallahassee with one of my homies only to watch it get shut down soon as we entered. I knew going forward we could not get "caught slipping". So, we began to load up and party in Tallahassee. On the contrary, Tallahassee parties were laid back compared to Quincy parties. The DJs would play more dance music instead of hood music.

I heard about the party scenes in Tallahassee, but I never really attended in Middle school. I drove to school in high school so I would scroll around the city when I got out of school to check out the neighborhoods, sides of town and connect with associates. Life changed in high school, for example, we purchased three cars, moved to the outskirts and I received a taste of financial freedom. This was a new experience for me.

Reflecting on a childhood memory, I remember I told myself I would never be ungrateful again. I came from this summer program called 21 centuries. I walked into the apartment complex office to a bag of clothes from Citi trends. Citi trends is a retail clothing chain selling discounted products to urban customers. I saved $40 from working over the summer in Fort Lauderdale to purchase clothes. My mother added money with it to get me some outfits for the summer program. Instead of me being grateful, I complained about her spending the money to get the clothes. I called them ugly and complained with the worst attitude ever. I watched her smile turn to cry and she threw the bag at me. I ran up to hug her, but the pain was already done. My auntie aims to explain to me the dynamics of the situation. I was very young at the time and times was harder. It was a few years after the divorce. I had everything I needed for school, etc. but I was following the trend. I was being materialistic and ungrateful because I was in an environment where kids judged you by your clothing. I am grateful my mother made sacrifices to put me in an educational environment with different values. However,

I was able to dress however I wanted to dress and drive in sport/luxury cars. The hate begins…

Coming from humble beginnings, I did not receive much hate growing up. People would dislike me because of my talent is areas. Sometimes, I would get called a "know-it-all", but it was not an abundance of hate coming from material things. The energy changed once I began to come to Tallahassee in the STR-8 charger, 7 series BMW, or the Expedition with 24-inch rims. I was not humble anymore. I would pull up with my gold teeth shining, new Jordan's and music blasting. People began to ask questions, they wanted to know where I came from. I did not attend any of the public schools, but I had a Myspace and Facebook. I grew to become popular in the areas, but the generational beef still exists. The Havana generation before us and Tallahassee has a brawl in the mall.

After a few calm parties and mall visits, we begin to attract the wrong attention. They realized we were from Havana and we had to fight our way into the city to earn respect. Tallahassee is a little different from Quincy. We would fight in Quincy and know we were going to fight the next time or until the beef was squashed. However, Tallahassee would be a fight one day, shoot out the next day, and fight again. It never seems to end. The environment was different. I will not disclose every fight; altercation and I will take most of it To The Grave. I was always great at separating school and weekend festivities. Yet, somehow a situation made it back to school. Long story short, I left FSUS and went to East Gadsden High School my sophomore year.

Arriving to East Gadsden High School on my brother Michael Gordon Birthright Day, I received a reality check. I was back riding the bus to school, eating school lunch, and the curriculum was not intense. The environment was completely different. I was around my neighborhood brother and sister. I recognized familiar faces from our 21-century summer program and parties. As I walked through the halls, I felt caged like an animal listening for bells and whistles. Sometimes, there would be an outburst of fights and everyone would run to record it. The school lunch was divided with limited food selection. The school was located in the middle of woods so you could not leave to go get food from anywhere else. I realized; I did not completely understand my previous opportunity because I wanted to focus on street life more than my education. I was making subconscious decision to allow my environments to control my actions. I've always been a leader without following. However, I was following in the big picture. I couldn't see it because I was making decision in the small pictures. This landed me in a school with a prison like setting.

I made a promise to myself. If I get another opportunity for a positive environment and promising opportunities, I would make the most of it. Shortly after, I was involved in an incident. A former associate began to taunt one of my brothers. I expressed the importance of staying out of trouble. Conversely, we both had reputations to keep so either we were going to handle the problem or lose earned reputation. Reputation was important because reputation could save you in life or death situations. Reputation was similar to currency growing up. If you had the right reputation, you could open doors nobody else could open. By the grace of GOD, the situation deescalated before we took the trained approach. The signs were clear. I did not belong there. This was not going to be a nourishing home for my academic, social, political, and economical success.

It was mandatory to relocate once again. I was a drop out for a few weeks. My tenth-grade school year required major adjustments. After a long transformation process, I was grateful to arrive to Amos P. GODby High school. The environment was welcoming. The teachers actually cared about our learning. The guidance counselors were skilled, listened and provided opportunities outside of our average curriculum. They spent their time listening and could relate to us even if they didn't agree with our course of action.

Florida State University School could not relate or understand my struggles as a young King growing up without close academic guidance. East Gadsden High School wanted to label me as a gang member and kick me out before giving me a fair chance at success. GODby High School accepted, embraced, and encouraged me to be a better student, man, and overall human. I would never forget my first teacher, the Honorable Yolanda Williams. Her energy was dynamic and powerful. She's the epitome of compassion and academic brilliance. She gave me a warm welcome with open arms. She broke every negative thought and emotion. I found a desk close to hers to gain as much knowledge, wisdom, and understanding possible. The school became another family to me. This was very important because during this stage of my life, I was facing an identity crisis. I needed guidance and support. I always had goals of graduating. Out of three sons, I would be the first to graduate high school. I was determined to break the generational curse. I was determined to lead by example. I knew walking across the stage would mean the world to my mother. She declared and spoke life over my intellectual abilities, promising future, and ambitions. Her expectations were clear, high, and persistent. It was not in my spirit to let her down.

I couldn't get a kick out of this school or leave early. The only option left would be going to Fort Lauderdale with my father and grandmother. It was not a bad option, but I already had a solid foundation here despite the obstacles and struggles. I already had a popular identity. I already earned my respect. I had everything I "needed". I enrolled week after a major fight. I made it very clear, I was not coming there to fight anyone. I was not allowing any beef to affect my education again. I only had one fight at GODby. After school, I was approached in the parking lot by a student. He aggressively bumped shoulders with me. He carried a beef from months, maybe years prior. One night my homies got into a brawl that lead to a shootout after a party in Quincy, Florida. These issues never seem to cease. I told him to meet me at Dade Street. It was a very simple response. I didn't want to create a scene on campus. I knew what I had to do. I went to get my brothers Dee Miller from James A. Rickards High School. Chad and Ko were inside the car with me. I felt it was going to be a possibility of us getting jumped so I got back up just in case. I told them to make sure it's a fair one on one. I did not want to start allowing this beef to continue, but I did want him to respect me.

Arriving to Dade Street, I jumped out the car. The music was playing Lil Boosie, "Set It Off". We fought a fair fight in the beginning.

Ko made sure it was a fair one backing everyone up with her tactics. My cousin Chad jumped over the back of a car and finished beat him down towards the end. He said, "I had to hit that N**** cousin." At the time, we didn't believe in one on ones even though that's what I requested. We squashed the beef. I did not have any more problems throughout the rest of my years at GODby. I later learned this behavior was considered dysfunctional. On the other hand, I did phenomenal my first semester. I earned 5 As and a B. I was back on track and heading to become a junior. I began to be recognized as a scholar again. I gained my academic identity back. I did not feel judged by the past and I began to feel appreciated for my character. I began to feel accepted and empowered. This was the birth of the inner greatness. My chemistry teacher had an intern from Florida Agricultural & Mechanical University, named Ms. Clayton. She always stayed on top of me because she knew I had the ability to turn in high quality work. Both of them held me accountable throughout the year. Chemistry Honors was the last class of the day, but this class was fun with phenomenal friends. Special thanks to Tryton Johnson, Markise McQueen, LeLe, and many more. I could not skip this class, but everyone would miss me in class.

Additionally, I got invited to attend the end of the year trip. Mr. Nicolas granted our class an opportunity to go to Philadelphia. I went to Disney world when I was younger with my Dad and family. I went to different water park thorough Florida with the 21-century program, but Philadelphia was far up north. The list was completely full, but Mr. Nicolas and Mr. Scott made a way. My mother and Ricky Jackson made sure all funds were paid so I could experience

Philly. I recently shared a picture on Facebook to tell Mr. Nicolas, "I'm forever grateful. The Philadelphia trip is at the top of my list. I was exposed to so much outside of Florida and Georgia. You get the coolest teacher award for this one." Why? Because when a child is exposed to see more, they aim to discover more. I grew up in an environment where individual struggle to make it thirty minutes to the next city and I received the opportunity to go to over 16 hours north as an 11th grader. We did a scavenger throughout the city, tried authentic Philly food, visited legendary monuments, and created lifelong memories.

Approaching senior year, I began to see the light at the end of the tunnel. My mindset was do or die. I began to see the product of hard work, consistency and relentless efforts. My guidance counselor, Mr. Darius Jones, put me up to a brave challenge. He saw I was succeeding in Honors courses, so he challenged me to take more AP courses and honors. I was prepared to accept the challenge. I really had to buckle down. I put forth full effort and maximized. The first semester was over. I looked at my grade point average, GPA, I had a 4.42. Building and maintaining a great GPA was the first step. The next step was understanding how to use it. Mr. Jones would read poems and make jokes to spark something inside of me. He had a great sense of humor. His sense of humor helps pass points across without much tension. I was very stubborn with a hard head, but I listened to him. I felt he genuinely had my best interest at heart. He actually has a book out titled, "Start over if you must but PLEASE don't quit." He still is empowering others and leading by example. My feelings about him were correct. He's a phenomenal individual. I received great tips, advice, and direction about scholarship opportunities.

This motivated me to apply for as many scholarships possible. Mr. Jones recommended countless scholarships. Soon as the scholarships arrive to the school, he would call qualified students out of class to give us an application. Mr. Zachary Ansley, assistant principal, recommended the Links Beautillion program. Mr. Ansley was known for chasing students down in the hallway to tell them to pull up their pants and lecturing them for two periods. Everyone had a love hate relationship with Mr. Ansley. He was like the school father. Instead of sending students home, he would converse with them to understand the root of the problems. After he understood the root, he would give us constructive criticism to help us think through the problem to find a solution. He was actually living faith, hope, love. He's one of the reasons I decided to go to Florida A & M University. He explained the significance of an HBCU, afforded opportunities, and aligned visions. Once he offered to allow me to do some lawn service work to help put some legitimate money in my hands. I might take him up on his offer now. I'm joking but he's really a great person. He saw so much greatness and potential in me.

He would play chess in the courtyard; he would call out students and play the best of the best. One day out of the blue, I sat down quietly and played him. He was talking without looking at the board, I did not say much. I moved with strategy without boasting. A few moves later, he began to sit down and pay attention to the board. However, it was too late. A few moves later, checkmate. Mr. Ansley told me, "I've never been beat out here before." I received a gift from him. I carry it with me to events, a traveling chess board.

My father, grandmother, brother and uncle taught me how to play chess when I was younger. They helped me understand chess is similar to life. Be at least three steps ahead and move with purpose. This core principles never left, and Mr. Ansley took me under his wing for the rest of my time there. Everything was smooth sailing. I established phenomenal relationships with my teachers and trusted the process. This was a major shift that changed the trajectory of my future.

June 28, 2013, I post a picture on Facebook stating, "I was heading to become a statistic fighting, shooting, etc. Lead by anger and driven by strong emotion. Anything I wanted I got it by any means necessary. Now I want to be successful, I understand to become successful you have to remove yourself from around negativity or anything that is holding you back from attaining goals. Nothing is wrong with clubbing, partying, or having fun but prioritize and accept responsibility. Don't let anyone deprive you from making it to the top because they are comfortable with the bottom. I received my Rattler Card yesterday and as I matriculated; I'm distancing myself away from negative people, places, or things. Graduation was the end of a hard-long road and college is the beginning to a new prosperous, promising life."

The purpose of disclosing this part of my story is to show at-risk youth their decisions, associations and environments can land them into situations. I'm not proud of any belligerent, ratchet, savage behavior. I do not promote violence or glorify negative learned behaviors. I'm sharing my story to let everyone know I was never perfect. I do not think I will ever be perfect. I only aim to be perfect in the eyes of GOD. I realized; a person is one decision away from living a completely different life. When I became exposed to more positivity and opportunities, I knew I wanted more. I took positive learned behaviors from my neighborhood and applied it to any environment I entered. Small-town ethics and neighborhood values are powerful when used properly. It was my imperfections that strengthen me along the journey to success. I experienced challenges, battles, and oppression at a young age. However, I experienced joy, perseverance, and survived. I developed character early. I began to develop a sharp sense of wisdom. I began to make positive decisions. I began to dream big. I began to understand the importance of a positive environment. I grew to be a great man of understanding and virtues. I developed to understand and embody the concept of "mind over matter." Here's a GEM: *It's not about where you start but where you finish.*

Some individuals understand and some may not understand. If you do not understand, maybe this book is not for you. My goal is to impact, touch, and inspire individuals to reach their full potential. My mission is to enlighten the mind, body, and soul of everyone who comes into contact with this book. The only way I can accomplish the mission is by being honest with my readers and myself throughout the process. I'm embracing vulnerability. I've had a meeting with individuals who are not aware of the struggles faced as a young African-American male, Gadsden county residents, or at-risk youth. I've communicated with individuals who simply don't understand our culture. I have a strong desire to bridge the gap. I'm tired of hearing about "the haves and have nots", we're all human. Each one of us have unique stories, gifts, and talents. Each one of us hold our own personal treasure.

I grew up without a biological father in the household. I was sexually abused and molested multiple times by different abusers throughout my childhood and adolescents. I learned most of "the game" on my own. I used to wear hand-me down. I suffered from mild depression, insecurities, and severe anxiety. I lived with untreated ADHD and PTSD. I took speech classes due to a speech impediment. I was bullied until I began to fight back. I endured many forms of oppression. I failed countless times. I was bruised and abused. I was denied opportunities based on my physical address. I was denied jobs based on my appearance. I was not polished or punctual enough in certain situations which lead to many insecurities. I feel my brothers and sisters of struggle who want more but do not understand the formulas or steps.

Additionally, I grew up in an environment full of love. I was blessed with a loyal, caring family. I established connections with great friends, supportive teachers and guidance counselors. I was influenced by positive OGS. We were willing to accept responsibility for each other. We were willing to share responsibility with each other. We come from a community where your word is your bond. In our struggle, we were taught to strive for education, economic, political, social development, and unity. Our community also had Community Resources for Independent People. I was surrounded by leaders and father figures. Every day I had nourishing food, clean water, cash, light, shelter, and other tools to persevere. My struggles did not meet everyone first. They usually meet my smile, great energy, and loving spirit. I was blessed and fortunate to grow up in this environment.

One of the most powerful tools I could have ever grown and developed was a positive enhanced mindset. A mindset to strive for greatness despite doubts, fears, or uncertainties. A mindset to have faith and trust in the process. A mindset to live each day to the fullest without complaints. A mindset to accept the things I cannot change. A mindset to change the thing I can. A mindset to gain the wisdom to know the difference. A mindset to be happy internally despite external influences. A mindset to love myself. A mindset to be confident. A mindset to feel accomplished and prestige. A mindset to develop into a King. A mindset to reach my full potential and develop into the best version of myself. A mindset to embrace my struggles.

I declare and speak you will utilize the concepts, philosophies and principles throughout this reading. I declare and speak you will reach into your gifts, tap into your purpose, and radiate your greatness. If I can do it, you can do it. I'm not different from anyone else. Some of the same struggles I face is behind the smiles of your friends, family and loved ones. The struggles might be behind your own smile. Struggles create winners. Struggles create champions. Struggles make you stronger. I declare and speak your struggles will transform into strengths. This transformation will not be easy.

You will experience times in the beginning when you will want to go back to your old habits. You will lose some friends as you grow and develop into the best version of yourself. You will create distance between some of the people you love the most. You will experience growing pains. You will experience discomfort. You will experience emotional and spiritual battles. It's necessary because your life matters. You will not become another lost soul. You will not be lost and forgotten. You will not become another failed statistic.

However, you will experience a promise filled life. You will find peace, love, and serenity. You will find acceptance and forgive those who caused you harm. You will become stronger. You will become enlightened. You will manifest great things into your life. You will attract people with pure intentions. You will be able to identify the difference between positive and negative energies. You will find yourself. You will continue to reach towards your full potential. You will continue to develop into the best version of yourself. You will gain consciousness. You will be purposeful in your action. You will be brave. You will be courageous. You will understand why you're doing things. You will think before you act. You will gain control over your emotions. You will think like the 1%. You will become the 1%. You will transform. You will reach your full potential.

FOUNDATION POEM

Everlasting Depths of Darkness by Patrice L. Delevoe Jr.
A 2013 creation from Mr. Nicolas 12 Grade AP Literature Class

Once there was a child with no feet

Innocence child, dark skin, deep scars

Lost in privation with no food to eat

Forced deep down in darkness to grow

No sun, no shine, just rain, pain, and shame

No name, no fame but darkness, lame!

Dark, dark, night, night nobody wants to hold it tight

Wishing, hoping, praying, fighting for better

Falling deep, deeper, and deeper in darkness

Red flames cast up as a light

Horns facing, devil holding his scythe.

Run, run, fall, fall, pray, pray, GET AWAY

Cries unheard, secret buried deep

Tears flow, Savannah creek.

Hurting pain, scared beneath.

Deeper and deeper. Everlasting Deep

FOUNDATION QUOTES

"For unto whomsoever much is given, of him shall be much required," –*Luke 12:48*

"Love is patient, love is kind. It does not envy, it does not boast, it is not proud."

It does not dishonor others, it is not self-seeking, it is not easily angered, it keeps no record of wrongs. Love does not delight in evil but rejoices with the truth . It always protects, always trusts, always hopes, always perseveres. Love never fails. But where there are prophecies, they will cease; where there are tongues, they will be stilled; where there is knowledge, it will pass away. For we know in part and we prophesy in part, but when completeness comes, what is in part disappears. When I was a child, I talked like a child, I thought like a child, I reasoned like a child. When I became a man, I put the ways of childhood behind me. For now, we see only a reflection as in a mirror; then we shall see face to face. Now I know in part; then I shall know fully, even as I am fully known. And now these three remain: faith, hope and love. But the greatest of these is love." –*1 Corinthians 13:4-13*

"GOD, grant me the serenity to accept the things I cannot change, Courage to change the things I can, And wisdom to know the difference." – *Mother Bathroom Wall*

"Focus on the hard times ahead with thoughts of those who came before you. Focus on the mission ahead with thoughts of your role as a leader in your community. Focus on the obligations of your family with thought of their needs first, personal needs last. Focus on the future of your people with thoughts of your course of action to make their dreams come true by any means necessary. "Yes you can" Become the… Thinker" – *Delevoes Lobby Office*

"Train up a child in the way he should go and when he is old, he will not depart from it." –*Proverbs 22:6*

"It's not about perfect. It's about effort. And when you implement that effort into your life. Every single day, that's where transformation happens. That's how change occurs. Keep going. Remember why you started." –*Anonymous*

"First comes thought; then organization of that thought, into ideas and plans; then transformation of those plans into reality. The beginning, as you will observe, is in your imagination." –*Napoleon Hill*

"I don't know what you're up against, I don't know what you're facing. But here's what I do know: You've got something special, you've got greatness in you, and I know it's possible that you can live your dream."
–*Les Brown*

"Be a leader, not a follower." –*Cheryl Delevoe*

Truth be told, everyone struggles. It's left up to you to find the value

SECOND EMERGENCY THERAPY SESSION

August 3, 2017
3:22am

Patrice L. Delevoe Jr.: I went to different tours as far as Howard and Morehouse and things of that nature, but as far as the college experience that I received on the tours, it wasn't as welcoming as FAMU. As far as the welcoming party, it was different types of students that took us on the welcoming tours, some came from a higher socioeconomic status, where they had Mom and Dad in the home, who had successful careers, and were able to cycle all of their child's college expenses into their budget. Then you had some that had both Mom and Dad who were not super rich, but they were still able to cover college expenses. Then you had students who came from a home where Mom was the only one providing college funding. So, for me…in my eyes… for me to go to school, I was aiming to get all of the scholarships that I needed to cover my tuition and to make things smoother for me to transition to college. I obtained a full scholarship to go to FAMU but not Howard. Howard and Morehouse are private schools, whereas FAMU is a public HBCU, so for Howard and Morehouse their tuition prices are completely different from FAMU. So, I looked at stuff like that as I considered which University to attend.

Patrice L. Delevoe Jr.: Once I got to FAM, I noticed people came from Chicago, Atlanta, down south, west coast, and different countries just to go to FAM, but as Tallahassee natives we look at FAMU like "Oh that's just FAMU", and a lot of locals that went there probably just go there because it's convenient. However, while choosing to attend FAMU for convenience, it was an inconvenience for someone else, but the inconvenience is worth it because somebody else can see the value in the programs at FAMU. So, it's like I began to go out there, look around, and just listen. As I did that, I realized they really had so much to offer. Their tours were not just explaining what they had to offer. It was so much diversity in all areas, and you could tell it was genuine. It was an environment that provided academic excellence and an opportunity to be socially active. It was undergraduate friendly. That was something that I didn't really get from the other college tours. I did see a little bit of the social side at Morehouse, but it was just a different culture. I do feel like I could have gotten a lot from going to those other Universities (Howard and Morehouse), but ultimately, I couldn't just leave my Mom. At the time, my middle brother was living in Hawaii and my oldest brother was never consistently in the house because he was in and out of jail, so as the baby boy, it's a different level of responsibility that you embody. So, I was not able to go too far away for college. Even if I went to college in Tallahassee, with my own apartment, I would never be too far away to go home (Havana, FL) to her if I needed to.

Jay D: I have "chosen one" tatted on me because I feel like out of all of the experiences, trials, tribulations, and testimonies that I have been through I'm the chosen one. Historically, if you look back on people who have made a big impact on society and the world, you'll see that it wasn't something that was done overnight. It was something that took more effort than efforts that keep you in the norm. It took greatness. It takes an extraordinary person and my whole life I have been aiming to keep that extraordinary part of me because it's like society will try to take that away and keep you in the box, make you think one way, causing you to not realize your potential in certain areas that are not commonly promoted in society—lose your creativity. I knew as the chosen one, you must wear that title with purpose. When you live with purpose, you allow life to guide you and you pray. As you are enlightened, you learn how to move a little better.

Jay D: On this arm *pointing to tattoos* it's an eye and city dreams, then you have blood sweat and tears. This right here (tattoo of a woman) represents the lust in the world. Right here *pointing to another tattoo* it says every saint has a past. Right here are money bags, representing money being the root of all evil. Right here *points at another part of the left arm* is a tattoo depicting gambling, corruption through music, and jewelry, but these things are only bad because of the materialistic value that people are attaching to these things, making them do ridiculous things. But the actual art of music and the craft of throwing dice, I don't consider it bad. It only becomes bad when the root of evil—money—comes into play.

Over here *points to the right arm* it's going to have tattoos that represents the conscience and peace. It's going to say every sinner has a future. So, it's like even if you are caught up in the mist on your journey between any parts on the left side, you can still find your peace over here *points to right arm*.

I feel like as I transitioned to go to college, it's like I was transitioning from one stage of my life to another and it wasn't easy. Even though I had the full ride scholarship to FAMU, my Grandma passed.

PJ: My grandma got sick and passed when I was in a character development program—Links Beautillion. Despite her getting sick, my mindset was *"work through your hard times"* but as I worked through my hardest times, to know my Mom was there with her, witnessing her (my Grandma's) condition getting worse and as I would talk to her I could hear her trying to be strong, but at the same time I know her…that's my Mom. As the youngest son and being so connected in our relationship, when she hurts, I can feel her pain. I was hurt that my Grandma was passing but I was also hurt from my Momma's hurt—the family's hurt. It was something that was a pain but also a source of motivation.

Growing up, I knew my Grandma as always being very healthy and active. She would work in her garden a lot. She was a strong woman and her presence was powerful yet respected. She liked things to be a certain way and if they were not, she would aggravate you until you corrected it. She would get on everyone, but you knew she loved you. She had the best sweet tea, food, and smile, but Grandma left.

-----BREAK-----

Jay D: During my senior year in high school, I was in the Links program, where I was awarded a $1600 scholarship. I was chosen by my peers as the best all-around beau, which awarded character, academic excellence, and embodied what it meant to be a Beau. I also received an award for having the highest GPA. I did not expect this award because throughout the program I would hear other students talk about college preparatory classes that they were in. I would hear them talk about their dreams and aspirations, so I assumed that their grades were very high, because that what it took to achieve their goals. However, my GPA that semester was a 4.42 because I was also in AP classes. Despite my high GPA, the award was still very competitive, so I didn't expect to win. Then I got another award for participation and commitment. I was one of the few who took on challenges of the program and stuck it out. The program also included an entrepreneur and community service components. For the entrepreneur part, we were given an assignment on figuring out how to recruit sponsors for an event, have sponsors set up tables, and raise money. I raised $1500.

I always wanted to be the best and dominate the competition, but as I got older, I realized it wasn't about dominating the competition it's about making a change in the most impactful and positive way. That program inspired me and empowered me to work through my hard times.

-----BREAK-----

Jay D: When I started at FAMU, everything was going well my first year, but then trying to separate my college life which was in the same city as my street life, it became difficult as I went to events that had a mixture of both. So, we had beef in the city. We were at the fair one night, and my little cousin ended up getting shot and he didn't make it. Two of my little cousins got shot, one made it, one didn't…RIP Chad. Everybody had been talking about getting out of the streets and making moves to live a better life, but we weren't really taking any losses to the point that it was hitting home. Like other people had friends that were passing. Like you see stuff going on but that wasn't happening to us. We weren't even taking any losses when it came to fights…other cliques would get beat up but not us. But that night Chad was killed, I left the fair early that night because when I balled up my first, where my knuckle is, my bone was coming out. Theoretically, there was a fight that night and my fist got split and even though there was blood coming out I did not realize my fist was split until after the fight was over. So I went to the hospital, and as I was at the hospital I received a phone call, and my lil homie, CJ, he called and was like:

CJ: "Bru…bruh…"

Me: "Man,wussup, man?"

CJ: "Bruh…bruh…bruh…bruh…Chad just got shot bruh! Chad and Joe just got shot bruh! I don't think Chad gone make it!"

Me: "What man…stop playing…ya feel me"

I hung up and got u off of the bed. The nurses were trying to check my pulse and all that. I got up and walked outside a little bit and logged on Facebook. You know Facebook is like WCTV live. I started seeing statuses.

I called back and he's like "I don't think he's gone make it". So you hear it on him (CJ). I'm at the hospital and the next thing you know people are pulling up to the hospital…Chad Momma…Ma. Muffin is breaking down, her sister, cousins, Joe's Momma, Ken's Momma, were all family. Your Momma is my Momma. My Momma is your Momma. That's just what it was. To see our Mommas hurt and to know that we were the last ones with Chad and Joe, and they are our jits … our responsibility, even though we were 18 and they were 16, we were older. I felt even more so responsible because I was the one that always made a case to our parents as to why they should allow us to go to a party, to the fair, or an event because we worked hard keeping our grades up and we deserved to go. Even though our clique was a group of young black males we prioritized good grades and held each other accountable for academic excellence. We had to be on our shit. You couldn't just be out there acting like there's no tomorrow. But with that, being that I was 16 years old driving an SRT-8 Challenger with 24s on it. My truck had 24s on it. I was a freshman driving to school. It came with a lot of hate. It came with hate from seniors and people in the city and that hate lead to fights. It used to be times that we would fight 2-3 times in one weekend and shoot outs would happen. All kind of things would happen but that was the circumstances and the environment that was present. When we would go places, if someone attacked you,

you defend yourself, and if defending yourself meant you'll had a gun and they had a gun, and somebody shot at you and you shot back, that's what happened.

Jay D: The only alternatives to school was going to a party or going to a celebrity basketball game, but that didn't change the hate that someone else had toward you. So, if a person tries to attack you just to report it to social media, you are required to defend yourself.

Jay D: For example, people would get into it on Facebook and say things like "when I see you I'm gonna slap you" or "when I see you I'm gone get off on you" or "when I see you, run me that" or "when I see you, I'mma get it up out you like however". So when you see each other at a big event, regardless of how many of us there were against them, what you said is what you said, and you are either going to do something about it or not and the same for them. But the way my mindset was, if you come in my face, I'm going to punch you in your face, because I already have an anger issue and you don't need to be bothering me because I'm not bothering you. This is my personal space. I had a zero tolerance to a lot of stuff because a lot of stuff was zero tolerance with me. So I was already conditioned, like if a nigga was talking sideways, and it seems as though he was actually going to attack me, I had to make sure I was straight. I couldn't come home after losing a fight and it be accepted. If I got beat up in the streets, when I got home I'd get a whoopin'. I was raised that if someone hit you, you know what to do. Treat people how you want to be treated but don't let anyone run over you. I was raised the old school way.

Jay D: I believe I have PTSD…post-traumatic stress disorder, meaning I am still mentally and emotionally suffering from a traumatic event that occurred in my life—the night Chad was killed. When I was at the hospital and they were putting stitches in my hand, the hospital staff didn't know Chad was my cousin, so they put us in the same room…in the bed next to me. While they were doing my stitches, they called his Mom and Dad in and you can hear them:

Chad's Dad: "CJ! CJ wake up boy! Wake up! Wake up!"
Chad's Mom: "My baby!"

Jay D: How do you hear that, you see that, you feel that? You feel me? That's your family. That's Ma, that's cuhh, you know what I'm saying? So you see your cousin laying there lifeless. This is your cousin that "right or wrong I'm with you". This is the cousin that said that night "everybody chill because we cool". He was the peace between the brawl and wanted the violence to stop and he ended up losing his life that night. From that point forward, there was just a lot of stuff that was done and said including me not being able to be as active in the funeral because people felt it was gang related, but at the end of the day my cousin was gone and we couldn't do anything about it at that time. We didn't even know who came through like that so we couldn't react or move on it in a forceful way, so we had no choice but to leave it in GOD's hands.

Jay D: Even though my mind understood that, my pain overpowered that logic, and I began to shut down. I went back in a shell. I didn't want to take any of my exams. I didn't want to talk to anybody, and I didn't give a f*** how anyone felt about that. That's just what is was. So, I begin to neglect my classes, my GPA dropped, and I lost all of my scholarships, but I knew I still had to pay to have somewhere to live. On top of losing scholarships, I was in a bad relationship, meaning when I became hurt and at my most vulnerable state I just needed to have an ear or a comforting shoulder or just a break away from what life was and I did not get that during the time that I needed it most.

Jay D: So, in an attempt to ease the pain, I would blow money and spend an excessive amount of money and then I would wake up and it was like ohhhh rent is coming up…rent is due. So, then I begin to think of ways that I could make money. I didn't want a job. Jobs weren't hiring me anyway, so I figured I had to start cookin'. I was cooking out of the house. I had different plates. On different days I would prepare different meals. I learned how to cook watching my Mom, my brothers, and my Dad. I remember one year my Dad made Thanksgiving dinner and it was so good. But my Mom always cooked…like throwed down. Whenever you would come in the house there was always cooked food—coming from school. I really learned how to cook when my brother began to have kids and it was required for me to cook for them. I also became motivated to cook when I was hungry, and my Mom wasn't home because she had to work long hours…double shifts and stuff like that. So, I was like boy you better learn how to cook boy. It's food in here. In my mind I was like Momma ain't here. You see how your brother cooks. You see where the stove is at. You know where the oil is at to make these pork-chop sandwiches. I learned how to cook pork-chop sandwiches very good. I learned how to get that season right…let it marinate. I learned how to cook burgers and fries. I use to love fries. I still love fries. I will eat me some fries. To have your fries with the ranch and ketchup. Some people might call that ghetto, but I like my fries with a little ketchup and ranch. I might want to chop up some pieces of chicken and put it in my noodles. That might be my luxurious way of eating my noodles, but you learn how to make a variety of foods by cooking one thing and mixing it in with foods that you already like to eat, so I was just learning how to mix up and try different stuff. Hell, there might be times where you didn't have any cream of chicken or cream of mushroom to make a gravy, so you need to make your own gravy from scratch. I had to learn how to do that. Grandma did it. Auntie did it. I come from a long line of great cooks. My Grandma, my aunties all of them know how to cook and bake well, so the natural ability was already there. It was just a matter of me getting connected with my own cooking abilities.

Jay D: So once I started to cook I started to generate income with Delevoe's Kitchen, but once the business took off people started reporting me. People started hating on me and reported that I didn't have the certification I needed to operate a restaurant from home.

Jay D: So, I just decided to get my face served and stopped operating the business. Back then I was so young. I made mistakes, but instead of people pointing out my mistakes and offering to help me correct them, they would be the people calling in to report me because that's just the society we live in.

Jay D: People are very, very, very, envious and hateful of one's success, even if they are supportive, ultimately sometimes people have a sense of jealousy that kicks in when a person is doing well and they are not benefiting. It's like a slave mindset or mentality. But I've been cooking for over 10 years.

PJ: I've been marketing for 14 years. I use to market my report card. When I got my report card. I would go show everybody how good my report card was (for money). I use to help sell candy for the church, "Hiiiii, I'm from Mornings Rock Ministry, would you support our church by giving a donation" and people would say "awwwwwe you're so cuttttttte" and I would be like "yes, I am cute ummmmm…..you know", but that's what it took.

PJ: Even though I am a grown man now, I'm still innocent in a lot of ways. I'm still that guy. The world can make you so corrupt, but it doesn't have to be that way.

That's why I aim to help everyone understand who you are and the importance of getting back to the roots of who you are…getting back to your happiest moments, embracing them, embodying them, and building on them. That's a mission that I have.

Ends Second EMERGENCY therapy session

2

PERSONAL GROWTH AND
SELF-DEVELOPMENT

D URING THE THIRD ANNUAL Links Beautillion my personal statement affirms: "I value integrity, honesty, openness, personal excellence, constructive criticism, continual self-improvement, and mutual respect. I am committed to giving back to my community and helping others in need. I value my personal relationship with my family, especially my wonderful mother: she has been a crucial component to the development of my character and achievement. She always warns me, "Never give up because the road ahead has long term benefits." Becoming one of the most influential African American Renaissance Men has always been a goal. Seven guiding principles help me transition dreams into reality: Be courteous; treat others with respect; embrace diversity as a critical component while doing business; apply the highest standard of excellence when stepping into any environment; contribute positively to the community; share personal experience with youth; and recognize that the three D's (discipline, dedication, and determination) are essential to future success. My plans are to be a businessman and psychologist. Recently, I was chosen 'Senior Superlative' for "best shoulder to cry on" when a peer is in need. I am active in the community donating countless hours to South Florida Leaders of Tomorrow, Riverside Apartments, and Havana Heights Apartments and a conscientious leader expecting to contribute to society by giving back and embracing the concept of service. One of my teachers always used a quote, "Never stop just because you feel defeated. The journey to the other side is attainable only after great suffering." I have faced many obstacles and adversity and each time I feel like a rock is on my back or a goal seems unattainable, I think about my teacher." My grandmother passed before the Beautillion; I remember suppressing my emotions to smile through the curriculum. I was learning valuable things such as etiquette, professionalism, golf, and many other valuable skill sets for an affluent individual. These values couple with positive principles currently motivate me to persevere through oppression. Life was not easy. Here's a GEM: *Work through your hardest times.* Most of my great accomplishments came with a fair share of struggles, battles, and obstacles. I am beyond grateful, a wise man once told me, "Life is dull without moments to test your strength and faith." I completely agree with this philosophy. Life begin to oppress me. Death was knocking at my front door, failure coming through the window and prison claiming my closest family members and friends. I began to feel lost. I turned 18 and moved out of the house with my mother. I wanted to experience life as an adult. I experienced getting money on my own and share household responsibilities. However, I didn't have the full responsibility.I received a full ride to Florida Agricultural & Mechanical University. The school was near my home and I could live off campus in a gated community ten minutes away. Some of my high school friends and Havana family lived in the same apartment complex. I was comfortable with the move. The first months started, and everything was going well. Our houses became a hub for everyone to play video games, politic and feel welcomed. I would tell myself, I would rather the family be here than out on the street doing something crazy. I always stood up for my friends when others would talk about them in a negative way. I remember my guidance counselors would express the power of friends and family. I told them; they didn't understand. Our family is different, we stick together and love each other. Nothing can come between the family.

On Wednesday nights, we would hit the Moon nightclub. DJ Demp, Tallahassee music personality and member of Ghost Town DJs and Cadillac Joe, King of Gadsden county DJs, would be on the ones and twos. It was always a live experience. Imagine a group of 15-20 + walking around the club, drinking and dancing like we own the club. Yep, that was me and the boys. Wednesdays was the college nights. Everyone would come from surrounding counties, colleges, and neighborhoods. I would introduce them to some of my college friends and we would hang out. I did a decent job of maintaining college and party life.

On Fridays, we would go to Pot Belly's, Coliseum, or any other party. Every day was another day to turn up and live life to the fullest. We would live like there was no tomorrow. I remember one night, a football player tried to fight one of the family members.

He swung and one of our big cousins hit him and knocked him out. These moments helped me realize something. I was one foot in, one foot out.

On Saturdays, we would get booths and bottles at Bajas. We were getting booths and bottles years before I graduated from high school. The loud music, dancers, sparkles from the bottles would always give me a rush. Everyone would be in designer clothes and go to the photobooth to flick it up. Tauris Patterson, owner of 850digital, would give deals on high quality photos. I still look at these pictures and reflect the times we shared. Some of us are dead, or locked up, but the ones out are doing exceptional. I always thank GOD for protecting us, strengthen us, and guiding us.

On Sunday, we would put in money to go to the meat market. We would grab some food and I'd cook. Family has always been a high value in my life. We would laugh, rap, joke like big families at a family reunion. Priceless moments. My closest cousin was locked up at this time. I always thought she would be home sooner than later. So, I didn't stress about it as much. I would've never thought these moments would be short lived.

The first semester was going decent. I learned to balance my life as a full-time college student, active family members, club promoter, and part-time retailer. I began to receive grades from my college courses. I was not doing well. I was not a failure, but I was not maintaining the GPA necessary for my full ride. I made a decision. I was dedicated time to studying and stay away from the party scene.

Approaching the end of the fall, many events happen. Homecoming, North Florida Fair, Car shows and other popularized events. I would take trips to fill my closet with designer clothing instead of shopping at the mall. I did not want to dress like everyone else. I wanted to look different, so I shopped in different places. Sometimes classmates would ask, "Where did you get that belt from?" I would respond, "If you want it, you can buy it from me right now." This began to be a common thing. I did not think much of it. I considered it a way to dress for free. I was not thinking about doing it full time as a business. However, I begin to build a reputation as a retailer. I became the designer plug.

My birthday approached so I decided the family and I would get a booth to celebrate. It was a few weeks since all of us went out collectively. I did not know this would be one of the last times all us would celebrate the way we did. I remember Chad recording a video for me as the bottles came out. The video is still upload on Instagram @DelevoeChapter16-21. Chad would always hype me up and uplift my spirit. Everything seem to flow again until one night I will never forget.

On November 15, 2013 – November 16, 2013 our families changed life forever. My emergency therapy session above states what happened to my cousins. It's not easy to write. It's is not easy to relive. It's one of the toughest and most traumatizing events I've experienced. This is the same for our family, friends and loved ones. Our life has not been the same since that day.

We did not receive any mental health treatments. When a loved one dies there's not a therapy or mental health account. We cope, deal, or function the best way we can. The family began to fall apart after Chads death. Some of us were there, some of us were not there.

Some of us pointed fingers, some of us tried to comfort each other. Some wanted revenge, some wanted peace. Some stuck together, some split apart. Everyone shed tears, everyone was heartbroken. I personally locked myself away from everyone. This was one of the first times I ever felt hopeless. If you ever lost someone close to you, you would understand this feeling. A feeling of emptiness in the middle of your chest. The thoughts in your head replaying everything vividly. The lack of appetite. Countless emotions.

I was influenced by older men and dudes I never saw cry. I always heard real men don't cry. This would turn my pain into anger. I would punch walls, yell, and breathe deeply to cope. I locked myself in my room for day. I remember I walked to my sister's house. She was located a building over. Somehow, I managed to drag my body across the parking lot. I slowly walked down the hall. I knocked at her door. She opened the door. I walked into her room and I fell to the floor. Every piece of pain I felt released at that moment. My heart was heavy. My little cousin was gone, my other cousin life changed forever. I felt responsible for everything because I was one of the oldest at the time. To this day, I still feel like they were my responsibility. I felt like I could have done or said something.

I had to be strong at the hospital for my mothers, Chad and Joe mother. I've watched movies showing everybody waiting until they hear something back from the staff. I just aimed to be as strong as I could. Our families were feeling the pain wholeheartedly. Every face had tears. The staff told us an hour or so later there was nothing they could do to save Chad. Screams and cries echoed throughout the emergency waiting room.

There are many parts of this night I have tucked away in my memories. There are parts of this night that I simply cannot disclose from my memory. The purpose of this book is to inspire and motivate others to reach their full potential. I do not want to relive these moments and fill this book with sorrow, pain, and trauma. It's been over 6 years, but the pain still runs deep to this day. The pain never leaves completely but you do find ways to persevere.

I made a promise to myself. I promised I would lead by example. I promised to never put my loved ones into situations or allow them to engage in violence if I can stop it. I blamed myself for my cousin's death for so long. I always felt like I should have tried harder to be a better influence. I was positive but I still had my fair share of adolescence problems. I just wish I knew what I know now back then.

As Chad's funeral approached, I was in a daze. I felt lost, puzzled, confused and didn't know what to do with myself. I was not mentally stable to lead anymore. I removed myself from everyone until the wake. I went to the wake and looked at him lying there. This moment reminded me of the moment Chad's mother, Muffin, and his dad, my big cousin, was in the back room with him. I heard big Chad voice saying, "Get up boy, CJ, CJ, get up boy." Then I could hear her voice saying, "My Baby... My Baby..." I felt like I was reliving the moment. As I write this right now, I feel a heavy weight, but I need for you to understand the emotions. Imagine getting stitches next to your cousin that just passed. Imagine hearing and seeing everything because the doctors do not know that's your cousin. Imagine feeling empty having an out of body experience. Imagine being 19 years old with the weight of the world on your shoulders without any problem situation. I was physically there but I was not there. I was checked out. I could not make this right. I just wanted my cousin back. He was a peacemaker. He was the laughter. He would always make a situation lighter than what it was. I miss you Chad. I promise I will not allow your death to go in vain. I love you cousin. I shed a tear writing this, but the world needs to know cousin. I know you are here with me in spirit.

Fast forwarding past depression, isolation, and academic failure, I found myself optimistically applying for jobs. In a short period of time, I was on the verge of losing my scholarships. My cooking business was not completely successful due to lack of proper management. My extended family was falling apart. My intimate relationship was failing. I began to feel lost. Life was testing my faith once again. I knew I had to become a success. I knew GOD did not bring me this far to drop me. I always smile on the outside but internally I didn't know what was going to happen. My faith was not as strong in my younger years. I leaned more on my own understanding. I knew I was not going to tell my mother I did not have a plan.

I would promote part time. Promotion was a decent hustle. However, club promotion is very competitive. I began to see it was a dog eat dog world in our club promotions. It was not a little boy game. It was extremely fast pace with individuals from all walks of life. I would sell booths, tickets, etc. only to make pennies on the dollar. I soon learned what to do to make this worth the time and energy. I would add my own bonuses to create a good profit margin. I would provide excellent customer service and move around like I was the owner. It was a cool night job. The most valuable skill sets learned was urban marketing, relationship building, and branding. Our club promoters are marketing geniuses. YepWeKan promotions, Wolf Pack, and 850 Digital took me under their wings and showed me how to street promote, college promote, and internet promote. They never were too specific. I don't even know if they knew they were taking me under their wing. YepWeKan would say, "Turn up on this event for me". Wolf Pack owner would ask questions, but he never really said too much. His partner, 850 Digital would say, "Get these flyers out for me and sell these tickets. You will make money from each ticket sell". I began to say less and observe more. Each had their own style of doing things. This created success for their companies. The principles and valuable skill sets stuck with me.

One afternoon, I received a phone call while sitting outside of my brother's house on Dover Street. It was WalMart in Tallahassee on Tennessee Street. They asked was I still interested in a cashier position. This was a breakthrough, I responded yes and proceeded to schedule an interview. I was excited to get my first job. I dressed up like I was winning an award at a banquet. I went to the back to speak with the manager. She hired me on the spot. I remember telling her, "I am a team player, responsible and dependable." WalMart located in Tallahassee, Florida on Tennessee Street. One of my close friends from Havana and GODby High School put in a good word for me. This was perfect timing because my lease was coming to an end at Park in midtown.

Instead of completely moving back home, I challenged myself. I always wanted to move into a luxury apartment. I wanted to be in a gated community away from everyone. I found the highest rated apartments near my job. This apartment complex had a deal for a $300 visa gift card, and I could move in within a week. I was sold. I proceed to sign the lease. Life was beginning to open up for me because I saw great things were possible even during hard times. I remember getting my paycheck and getting items for my apartment. I wasn't happy with the amount of my paycheck, but it was something to help out. I didn't have to ask anyone or do anything crazy to make money.

I put my all into being a cashier, I worked outside pushing carts and filled in wherever. However, I realized my pay only reflects the number of hours I work. The pay checks did not reflect the amount of work I put in. This was disappointing. I remember the days when I would work for the church, cooking plates, and other entrepreneurship duties. It was not adding up anymore. I felt devalued. I woke up one morning late with a hangover. Usually, I would make myself go despite my feelings. I just laid there. I know it was a better way.

I knew I was going to lose my job. I was not passing my 90-day temporary hire period. This was a no call, no show. This is not acceptable. I was not completely worried. I became a no call, no show in my real life outside of a minimum wage job. I was aiming to figure life out without a complete plan. Reflecting back, I recognized it is a recipe for disaster.

As I began to fight through the rest of the semester, I noticed I did not receive any scholarships. I did not have a job. My toxic relationships were not making anything better. I actually had two relationship and half way in another one. It was very comforting to have someone that could take my mind away from stress. Until the person begins to add to your stress or become one of your stressors.

One of classmates, Keviron Rollins, introduced me to this lifestyle enhancement company. He explained how the company focuses on personal growth and self-development. I was only 19 year old. He picked me up and we went to BJs restaurant. On the way to the restaurant, we were listening to an audiobook called The Secret by Rhonda Byrne. The Secret began to cause a mental Mindshift. Weeks before he came to meet me, we had a conversation via Facebook:

Coach Rollins: "First book I would prefer you to read is The Secret ... It speaks on The Law of Attraction"

PJ: "Okay I'm about to look into it now."

Coach Rollins: "This is what going to set you aside from everybody else ... You're different PJ and you're not like everyone else. You're a leader and I see it in you. It's time to take business and anything that you're trying to pursue to the next level! I'm going to be buying books and adding on to the library periodically."

PJ: "Thanks for the commendation. Being a leader always came naturally. I have no problem with respecting my surroundings and authority. However, I have free will and I'm going to use it. Most people are afraid of walking or taking journeys alone. It's nothing wrong with it because eventually you'll meet someone that's going or had been where you're trying to go even if it's in a different sense. I observe though bro and I'm on a journey towards the light. May people question why I hung with the people I hung with but to be honest you will never understand the struggle or poverty at its peak when you haven't been in it or seen it first-hand. I been through it, seen it first hand, and seen the pros and cons. The stories and experiences I have gained in the field of hanging and doing crazy things with my friends have prepared me for people in my profession. I will be able to relate and build connection from the foundation I build. A lot of people don't understand or see my vision. It's risky but anything you do that's worth something is going to have risk attached."

Dr. Rollins: "What are your plans to getting to the top?"

PJ: "Traveling and networking while I'm in school now. Building connections with powerful people. After graduation I plan on working a few years in a major city to save money and study the markets. I'm going to open a few franchises in continually growing areas. Invest money into stock. Once I create my residual incomes, I will venture off from working for others. I will invest more into myself and connect with those powerful people. Once we connect, they will become team of investors. I'm going to open an agency for the entertainment industry as their financial advisors, managers, consultants, and life coaches. In addition, I'm going to write books sharing my untold stories and experiences. I'm going to empower my friends using their life stories. I'm going to use my knowledge from working in the field and my experiences to train, coach and guide my employees. I have many more plans but like a magician I never reveal all my tricks."

I finished listening to the Secret after we had our dinner. Kev has always been a phenomenal business friend and leader. He was an influential athlete at Florida State University School. This characteristic resonates throughout his business ventures, etc. He greatly influenced me to start and finish the book. Somehow, I managed to listen to the secret within a day. To be completely honest, I never took the time to finish a book prior to audible. I would start and stop. I would read enough information to complete my projects or answer questions. This time was different, I was truly motivated. Within the 30-minute drive to the restaurant and back, I received much needed confirmations and affirmations. The secret revealed the Law of attraction. The three steps of the law of attraction are asking, believing, and receiving.

I realized a few things after listening to the secret. I was attracting many things into my life. I was attracting the great and unfortunate thing. The universe supports my thoughts by making these things. I began to see life was not hard or a struggle. Life is actually easy, and all good things will come to me. However, I have to feel it within myself. This was a game changer for me. I began to think about times I used the secret unconsciously. I began to think about times I did not want something to happen. For example, I would not want to get pulled over by Police. Then, I would randomly get stopped for the oddest reasons. The brothers and I would go out to party and we would say we did not want to get into a fight. Moments later, we are throwing chairs and elbows. We were literally attracting things into our life subconsciously. The strong feeling inside was attracting more into our life.

I began to reflect over my past. I wondered: did I really attract all the unfortunate events? Did I attract multiple sexual molestations and physical abuse? Did I attract poverty? Did I attract my heartbreaks? Did I attract fights and shootouts? Did I attract my parents' divorce? Did I attract bullying? Did I attract near death experiences? I lived for so long carrying the weight of my struggles like I was the cause of each of these events.

My sexual molestation and abuse started at the age of four. Yes, I was a four-year-old child. How could I be the reason someone I looked up to and trusted touched and abused me throughout my childhood? How did me wanting to play a video game lead to me performing sexual activities? How did wrestling lead to sexual activities? Why I couldn't sleep without getting touched or waking up to sexual activities being performed on me? One could say I knew right from wrong but in my developing and ideal mind, I thought this is what older kids do. One could ask, "Why didn't you tell?" It would have been so embarrassing to be the little boy in the neighborhood project or school who got raped. At a young age, I knew I did not want that to be a part of my identity. Additionally, I didn't want my parents or any family members to go to prison behind killing my abusers. Little did I know; my innocence was being taking away and

I would never look at life the same. The appearance of my teachers, elders, even other peers changed.

From birth to the age of fifteen, I was raised in the neighborhood projects. Based on statistics, it's considered poverty. Conversely, the culture is rich in-it-self. I learned how to be tough. I became a relentless warrior. I adapt strong values and principles. As I became exposed to different cultures and environments, I noticed our strengthens and weaknesses. Our resources are not plentiful, so we live in scarcity. Our resources are not plentiful, so we value our treasures. We can literally lose our life to jail or streets, so we live every day to the fullest. Our living to the fullest can be partying, dancing, and making the most out of a stressful day. We make the struggle look phenomenal. We aim to maximize every opportunity to the best of our ability. We are not bad, but a lot of us are misled and counted out. My location became my identity. This is the unfairness when coming from the poverty neighborhood projects. We are prejudged before any opportunities are presented due our generational challenges. My mindset has enhanced due to the technology advancements, information overload, and nourishing environments. My heart is still with the neighborhood project babies challenged with anger, doubts, fears, and struggle beyond intellectual thinking. I've been there. I've faced it. I've seen death face to face. I don't know if I'm attracted to it, but I thank GOD for it. Here's a GEM: *Pressure form diamonds.*

I fell in love so many times I lost sight of my own heart. This deeper than rap. I fell in love with a young lady who embarrassed me daily, talked to my best friend, and talked to me every night. I fell in love with young ladies who would kiss on me but began to like other ladies. I fell in love with girls who had sexual intercourse with my closest home boys. I fell in love with thick girls who told me about other dudes and I still loved her. I even fell in love with my therapist and I think she thinks I'm half gay. I just use to fall in love with people. My little heart has been shattered, broken, stepped over but it will not stop loving. I'm cracking up, laughing, over here as I'm writing this book. I'm completely kicking vulnerabilities behind and making it my female dog. Thank you Brene Brown and Lisa Nichols. The process of falling in love with each one of these individuals helped me understand parts of myself. Whether it was childhood love or adult love, it was the same for me. I still don't know if I attracted it, but I genuinely tried to be the best I could be to each one of them regardless of my struggles, battles, fears, and transgressions.

Honestly, I am real enough to say some fights were results of my thoughts. I would enter a state of mind, lower my frequency, and negative actions would transpire. Before fights, I would think about some of the worst things possible. I was fighting the other human but mentally I was fighting life itself. I was fighting everyone that talked about me. I was fighting myself. I was fighting spirits. I was fighting to keep reputation. I was raised to have integrity. If Jay D told somebody, "I'm going to see you when I see you.". Jay D had to see them when he saw them, he didn't want to talk. Jay D was about action. This attracted shootouts and other life experiences. Jay D didn't think about law of attractions in a negative way. Jay D was focused on attracting respect, authority, and power. While typing, I found a new GEM: *The law of attraction will bring the main attraction and things positively attached to it.* Imagine placing metal items on a table such as iron, nickel, and cobalt. Now, place a magnet in the center of each. If the magnet is large enough in size, it will attract each metal item. This is how the law of attract work. I wanted respect, authority, and power with a lack of wisdom, knowledge, or understanding. So, the result was fights, shootouts, and wars.

After talking to both of my parents, I recognized their divorce was not influenced by me. As a child, it's natural to assume problems are a result of your behavior. This is not an inaccurate perception. For example, if a child rides a bike and fall it's usually due to a lack of skill, attention, or malfunction. If an older child urinates in bed while sleeping, it's usually because he or she did not use the bathroom before getting into bed, drink something before sleep, and so forth. In each example there's positive correlations. So, based on things I controlled as a child such as riding a bike or urinating in bed, I began to associate the divorce with other things I controlled. This was a mistake. I was not old enough to understand the dynamics of a relationship. This helped me understand a powerful GEM: *Some-things are beyond your control. Accept it and move on.*

Growing up, I got bullied for some of the most ignorant things I could imagine. I will identify three forms of bullying I experienced. Verbal bullying because my name is Patrice. My name derives from Patrice Lumumba. Patrice was the first Prime Minister of the newly independent African state, The Congo. He was a fellow hero to Africans because he was the man who won his country's independence from the Belgians. He became a threat to western powers and became a target. In December 1960, Patrice Lumumba and two of his Ministers were assassinated by Belgian Secret Service. My name is phenomenal, it's attached to a great legacy. This was one alongside being picked at for my dark skin, heavy weight and high-pitched voice until I started using what I was taught in the neighborhood projects. In early grade school and middle school, I experienced social bullying. I didn't have the latest Jordan's, so I wasn't considered "cool". When I got in high school everyone wanted to be my friend because I looked like money. Individuals can be so fake so watch out for the snakes. Sometimes rumors would spread, and people would tell others not to be my friend. My own "friends" talked about me in my truck making gay jokes about me and didn't think I knew. A few of them told me individually like they were not involved. I was going to as for the fade, one on one fight, but I let it go. I charged it to the game. Children even went as far as trying to physical bully me because I was smaller. However, I was Trained To Go upside their head if they put their hands on me. I'm laughing out loud again but I am so serious. On a serious note, as a child these are serious issues. I would isolate myself. I used to think something was wrong with me. I wanted to be "normal". I will ask GOD himself how did I attract those issues because it's beyond me.

From birth, I have been experiencing supernatural phenomena. My mother told the doctors I was doing flips. They did an ultrasound and I turned breech during the pregnancy, only 3%-5% of births are breech. My mother was rushed into surgery to save both of our lives. The birth was a success. This was my first near death experience. My second near death experience was during an asthma attack. I was at my GOD mother's house. I felt my shortness of breath. Experiencing an asthma attack is very traumatic. I did not have my pump. They did not call an ambulance immediately, but they decided to call when my wheezing increased. They placed a hot rag over my face. I tried my best to make every breath count. I didn't know which one was going to be my last. Eric Thomas dropped a GEM when he said, "*When you want to succeed as bad as you want to breathe, then you'll be successful.*" The ambulance arrived, they rushed to split my shirt to get access to my chest. I stopped them with the little energy I had left. I told them, "My mom will get me and you about my shirt. I like this shirt." They told me they would get me another one. I passed out. I remember being in a large field as they rushed me to the helicopter. It felt like a dream. I was getting my first helicopter experience. I woke up to a bright light, my mother was in the room. She beat the helicopter to the hospital. They told her they were working on me. I was unconscious. They revived me. Did I attract this to me? Did the bullets miss me on accident? Some of these questions will never reach a conclusion.

On the other hand, I did attract greatness. There have been many opportunities for me to quit on myself. Instead, I attracted strength and resilience. I experienced many things on my journey, but many were concealed in my memories. Reflecting has helped me respect my tenacity. I did attract a full ride scholarship and high school graduation. I was the first and only son of three to walk across the stage as a graduated. This accomplishment alone was a win for our family. Receiving a full scholarship was the icing on the cake. This was attracted intentionally because I worked towards these accomplishments every single day. I did attract a loving and supportive family. I aimed to keep the morals, principles, and high standards instilled in me as a child. I often see individuals who are disconnected with their families. I aimed to make sure we stay connected despite differences. I did attract knowledge, wisdom, and understanding. I studied, researched, and applied as much as I could to gain these pillars of life. I did attract mentors, guidance counselors, father figures, finances, and protection. I wanted to get life right. So, I made a decision to get life right. I wanted to be better than my past. I wanted to actually make something out of myself. I was in the world but not of the world. This helped me understand and embody this GEM: *Past experiences are beyond your control, but you have the power to control your perspectives, actions, present, and future.*

Under all those circumstances, I was proud to become a young man of phenomenal character. I learn not to judge a book by its cover. I learn to attempt understanding the pages, content, and background of the book. The human who is fighting could simply be defending themselves to the best of their understanding, trying to fit into a social environment, battling with transgressions, or aiming to be acknowledge for something. The shy human could have possibly experienced trauma, suffers from insecurities, feels out of place, or needs a boost of positive energy to help break the ice. The human who does not wear the latest shoes or clothes could have parents who focused more on their educational and household needs, set their own trends, or carry different values all together. The human who is getting bullied might turn around to hurt you, empower you, save your life, or even write a book for you to read later. The near death experiences the human endured could have dramatically changed them, blessed them with wisdom, and accelerated their growth. The human who looks nothing like you could be facing similar battles, share parallel life missions, and/or can help you get to the next levels. The human from poverty, neighborhood projects, or struggle could be the next human to make a phenomenal impact in the world, save your life, or help you get past a tough time in your life. I learned to stop selling other humans short due to a lack of understanding. Here's a GEM: *Life and death is in the power of the tongue.* One thing for certain, neither of us will escape death, so let's continue to speak life to each other while we are granted this borrowed time.

As a living testimony, I have been on both sides of the fence. I have been the book. I have been a judge. I have been through many storms. Nevertheless, I came out of each storm developed into a new person. There have been many times I wanted to give up. I have a legit reason to quit. I could have given up without blame. I could have laid around in depression, held back due to hidden fears, talked about my stories in ways to gain sympathy, and so forth. As the chosen one, I followed one of the oldest philosophies in the book. I adopted this GEM: *That which does not kill us, makes us stronger.* Winston Churchill once said, "Success is the ability to move from failure to failure without loss of enthusiasm." We are all fighting with struggles. I pray we make it through each one. I'm confident anyone who has faced any similar inspirational trauma or even worse will grow and develop into the best version of themselves. I'm going to provide some helpful strategies for you.

Releasing Negative Energy

This exercise can be repeated as often as needed. It will help you tap into your greatest, unlock your full potential, positively use your inspirational traumas, examine your heartfelt life experiences, and break away from generational curses. This exercise may create a sense of discomfort initially. However, I want you to work through it to break free. Separate yourself from any distractions, unpleasant noises, and interferences. Say, "I am a survivor." Repeat this affirmation until you wholeheartedly agree. This exercise will require you to dig deep within yourself. Get six sheets of paper, writing utensils, and a device to access YouTube.

Find a quiet peaceful environment. Access YouTube and search, "Positive vibration frequencies", "Concentration frequencies", or "Release negative frequencies". Find a frequency with phenomenal ratings and reviews. The comments are usually very uplifting and inspiring. Feel free to comment and connect with a positive community. Close your eyes for a moment and focus on your breathing. This would help clear your mind for the exercise. Let's begin…

Reflections

1. Reflect on moments when you faced tough times…
2. Reflect on moments when you felt like giving up…
3. Reflect on moments when you cried until you could not cry anymore…
4. Reflect on moments when you carried guilt, shame, or deep remorse…
5. Reflect on moments when you were hurt by someone you love…

6. Reflect on moments when you wanted to express yourself but didn't…

In the front top right corner, label each sheet of paper with the reflection numerical value. On each sheet of paper write and explain the feelings received from each reflective moment. Do not judge, filter, or beat yourself up about how you felt. It's okay to acknowledge your emotions. This exercise will help you take control of your feelings and emotions. Often, we suppress our thoughts internally. We suffer in silence without allow energy to release. I believe this is very unhealthy and leads to depression, anxiety, and other stress related issues. This exercise will help you release negative energy by embracing your vulnerability and change your perspectives.

Positive Thinking

1. Think about how you grew from these times…
2. Think about how you keep pushing and survived…
3. Think about how you felt after you let it all out…
4. Think about what you learned from the situation…
5. Think about what you learned about yourself…
6. Think about what you wanted to tell them…

Find each sheet each sheet of paper with the positive thinking numerical value. On each sheet of paper with the same numerical value, flip it over and explain using positive thinking. Remember, "Life is 10% what happens to you and 90% how you react to it." The mission for this assessment is to help you change your mindset. I want you to try this over and over until your mind automatically thinks positive. If you always have a positive reaction to the 10% of what happens in life then the remaining 90% is positive. If 10% of events are negative with 90% positive reactions, you still would have an A for a positive life overall. That's phenomenal.

I learned thoughts determine frequencies. Frequencies will either manifest more events into your life or cancel them out. How many times have you woke up feeling bad? Did your morning seem to get worse? Someone irritates you. More unfortunate events continued to happen throughout the day. This is because of negative frequencies. Negative frequencies attract negative events. I learned to think positive thoughts to raise my vibrations thus increasing my frequencies. Here's a GEM: *Positive frequencies attract positive events.* There are many tactics an individual can use to increase their frequencies.

For example, many proactive individuals physically workout daily. This increases their frequencies. When you run or even jog it increases your productivity. If you watch someone who works out or stays active frequently, you rarely see them depressed or sad. When frequencies increase a series of great events occur. Days flow in harmony with your positive thoughts. I began to practice positive thinking. I attracted more positive events daily.

This Secret was the perfect book during this period of my life. I was spiraling back into depressed from lack of employment, possible criminal record, flunking out of college, and failed businesses. I was continually thinking about all the losses. I was thinking about the disappointments. I was thinking about the many sacrifices made for me to excel. When you're going through it without solutions, it's easy to think negatively or even lose faith. Nevertheless, the universe (GOD) was preparing some great things. I've learned over the years to trust the process because the universe (GOD) will work miracles. Once I understood the power of positive thinking and the law of attraction, it was time to manifest some great things once again.

I thought to myself, I've been manifesting things all along. I've manifested meaningful friendships, supportive clients, a luxury lifestyle, traveling experiences even mentors. I manifested a full ride to college, a few thousand dollars, even protection. I was not doing this consciously. I was determined to make things happen, but I was not consciously doing it on the level the book discussed. I had to consciously move from poverty thinking to abundance thinking. This transformation would take me on a journey towards my personal legend. I took every drop of energy and pour it into my new positive mindset. As I applied this ancient knowledge, I set out to reach my full potential despite my struggles.

PERSONAL GROWTH & SELF DEVELOPMENT POEM

The man in the Mirror
by Patrice Louis Delevoe Jr.

As I walk into the bathroom to see what was there

The mirror reflected pain & gave me a blunt stare

Seconds past by as tears began to flow

Once again, I have been brought to this hole

The empty place from deep within myself

Darkness filled, helpless help

Glaring at the insecurities from my past

And the misunderstandings that I once had

I punched the mirror and shattered the glass

Then I began to question how things got this way

But as I pondered, I felt self-hate

From the darkness of my skin, the pitch of my voice

The spelling of my first name, it was not my choice

Sometimes it was deeper, I just could not rejoice

To deal with my hate, I poked and pitched

I bullied and fought, even patronized kids

In them private school, I felt they deserved it

Became an outcast but I was just being me

I noticed we lived different realities

A friend I was trying to be

But my circumstances drove me to be their enemy

So, I isolated myself, focused on self-wealth

Self-health, self-worth and self-in-self

'F*** a friend, cuz ya dawg gon cross ya in da end'

I listened to that Plies over and over again

As I got older, I began to come out of my shell

Figured I'll try to be friends with someone else

Got a click who reminded me of self

All from broken homes and no one else

Hood niggas with dreams and street wealth

At least that's what I felt...

We got close and became a family

See we lived the same reality

Project babies, pork and beans

Candy ladies, and running the streets

But I didn't know it was another part of me

Attending them private schools, I was introduced

to three story houses with presidential views

to designer clothes, and cars with panoramic roofs

Even kids that was fed with a silver spoon

Now I wanted to be boss, I want an Audi coupe

Just have to figure out what I have to do...

See I realized I was a product of my decisions

Not my circumstances...

I understood I could be anything I want to be

Just got to do my best with the cards GOD hand me

Timeout for self-pity, enough with slave mentality

I am that, I am a man and you will see...

Standing over the sink in the broken mirror

That was full of broken glass blood, sweat, and tears

A strong man was born...

I smiled and walked away

And I never hated myself from that day.

PERSONAL GROWTH AND SELF-DEVELOPMENT QUOTES

"Do not believe in anything simply because you have heard it. Do not believe in anything simply because it is spoken and rumored by many. Do not believe in anything simply because it is found written in your religious books. Do not believe in anything merely on the authority of your teachers and elders. Do not believe in traditions because they have been handed down for many generations. But after observation and analysis, when you find that anything agrees with reason and is conducive to the good and benefit of one and all, then accept it and live up to it."
–Gautama Buddha

"If the only tool you have is a hammer, you tend to see every problem as a nail." *–Abraham Maslow*

"Beauty lies in the eyes of the beholder." *–Plato*

"The ends you serve that are selfish will take you no further than yourself but the ends you serve that are for all, in common, will take you into eternity."
–Marcus Garvey

"Personal development is a major time-saver. The better you become, the less time it takes you to achieve your goals." –*Brian Tracy*

"Investing in yourself is the best investment you will ever make. It will not only improve your life; it will improve the lives of all those around you." –*Robin Sharma*

"You won't get much done if you only grind on the days you feel good." –*Grant Cardone*

"Courage starts with showing up and letting ourselves be seen." –*Brené Brown*

"The seed that fell among thorns stands for those who hear, but as they go on their way they are choked by life's worries, riches and pleasures, and they do not mature.

But the seed on good soil stands for those with a noble and good heart, who hear the word, retain it, and by persevering produce a crop." –*Luke 8:14-15*

"Live life on purpose with purpose." –*Patrice L. Delevoe Sr.*

3

INSPIRATIONAL TRAUMAS

F REDERICK DOUGLASS ONCE SAID, "If there is no struggle, there is no progress. Those who profess to favor freedom and yet deprecate agitation are men who want crops without plowing up the ground; they want rain without thunder and lighting. They want the ocean without the roar of its many waters." (1857) After digesting a plethora of YouTube videos and audio books, I had an epiphany like T-Pain. I was struggling without making progress. My struggles to win at life began to weight down on my spirit. I felt myself losing strength to carry on. I would take one step forward, only to get knocked back three steps. I was coming to the end of a failed semester. My Ford expedition head gasket blew. My private relationship was coming to an unexpected end. I was getting arrested as an adult for the first time. My "friends" were stealing from my apartment again. My safe was emptied. Eviction notices begin to pile on my door. My emotions spiraled as I thought about my arrested family members and deceased cousin. My depression and anger began to resurface. The struggles and lack of progression was due to my toxic mindset, tainted environment, bad eating habits, negative thinking patterns, and unapplied knowledge.

I neglected listening to the books with consistency. Nothing was making sense anymore. I began to feel unguided and lost again. I was not applying the learned concepts and knowledge. I relapsed. My 20th birthday approached. I celebrated the night before, but the actual day was the first birthday I spent unaccompanied. This was the breaking point of my surreptitious relationship. I realized; I could not continue to pour into a leaking cup. On the other hand, I could always count on my mother to brighten up my day. My mother was at work when she contacted me to come visit her. I drove there to see her with a bright smile. She surprised me with some of my favorite gifts and much love. Prior to pulling into the driveway, I threw my phone across the car after reading another excuse from my addiction. The phone shattered upon impact. My energy was not uplifted at first. However, she eventually produced some authentic grins out of me. She's always been phenomenal at elevating my mood. I departed and head back to my lonely apartment.

I arrived back at the apartment front door, twisted my key, and dragged myself inside pass the doormat. I took a few staggering steps inside. I took a shot straight out the closest bottle I could find on the kitchen counter. I began to stand in the gloomy living room taking shots. I glanced at the pale walls and pondered on my impulsive, uncontrolled and emotional decisions. Reflecting back, I made myself a laughing stock among my friends. One even said, "That's what you get for putting your hands-on people." I thought my closest friends would be more encouraging, but they didn't even take it seriously. It had become a classical condition for the boys to accept jail or prison sentences without collective grievances. It was becoming a normal thing amongst us. I knew one of my charges carried up to 5 years imprisonment and the other carried a life sentence. This moment helped me understand the capacity of my decisions.

I began to realize life is truly about decisions. It's easy to overlook situations and allow them to become a bigger issue. However, I took the initiative and contacted an attorney after the officer contacted me to investigate the case. I needed great representation to tell my side of the story. I had a lot to lose even though I felt like I had already lost so much. I realized threats do not give you the right to defend yourself before a person takes action against you. I also realized; everyone does not come from the same environment. Everyone does not resort to violence even if they make threats. By the grace of GOD and my protective mother, one of my charges got dropped and one was reduced. I will forever love Anabelle Dias for accepting my case and representing me. She helped my brother Redd, Tallahassee Southside mayor, regain his freedom. He now owns and operate a barbershop called Clippers. She helped my brother Luis Guerrero, self-taught gourmet chef, regain his freedom. He owns and operate Great Plates Restaurant. She's truly a pillar in our community. She's known for helping many others gain second chances at life. I'm grateful she was able to help. However, I must admit the situation was a tough life lesson for me. I went to jail with a bond. I was in confinement because of my charge. I remember asking for a sheet of paper and a pencil. I thoughtfully wrote a few prayers, a letter to myself and poems on there. As I laid on the hard bed, I could hear my mother's voice, "You make your bed hard, sleep on it."

The next morning, I had first appearance. I was in a holding block with a few other guys. The guard tossed us some peanut butter and jelly sandwiches. Years later, I realized I was in the cell with a multimillionaire. He was sitting across from me. He faced a murder charge. His case was actually featured on a television show, years later. I wondered why cameras was out in the courts, but I didn't give it a second thought. Reflecting back, this moment taught me that everyone makes choices. I recognized even at one of the lowest points of my life, I was still rubbing elbows with millionaires. Nevertheless, at the end of the day wealthy or financially challenged we were in the same position. Fighting for our freedom. I just had to make sure the choices I make from this point moving forward were positive and impactful.

The judged called my name, read my charges and granted me a bond. I looked to my left-hand side and saw my family. My mother, brother E.T., sister Crystal and former girlfriend Quet Renee were there. I was disappointed to let them see me behind bars. I didn't see any of my friends or associates. I didn't see the person who planted seeds for me to get this charge. Thoughts went through my head, "I'm supposed to be different. I'm not supposed to take my mother through this cycle again. She's been through enough of this…". I sure was happy to see them there though. This moment was a stern reality check.

Once I was released, I walked outside the gates. I checked to see if anyone was outside waiting for me, but I didn't see anyone. My phone was dead so I couldn't call anyone. I walked from the jail to my apartment. The sunlight and a gust of fresh air rubbed my face and pushed my head up. This was a walk with GOD. I remember conversing with my Dad and Grandmother about being in the will of GOD. I recalled them planting seeds about going to church and praying. I heard them but I wasn't completely listening. I still wanted to do whatever I wanted to do. I thought I had everything figured out. I thought I was one step ahead of everything. I didn't see this coming.

I stepped up the stairs and arrived at my apartment door. I charged my phone and called my mother. I told her thank you for bonding me out and promised to stay on track. She found a way to speak life into me and told me to stay focused. I was ashamed. GOD was in the process of humbling and molding me. I was still ashamed because I did not understand. I thought GOD didn't like me anymore. I began to think about problems from my childhood. I began to think about every single, negative and traumatizing thought possible. Later that night, I could not take it anymore. I broke down. I was in the house alone, again. I was hyperventilating. I felt a heavy weight on my back. My chest felt so empty inside but tight. My head was throbbing. My thoughts began to run in rapid cycles. I started throwing things around. I began to punch walls. Suddenly, I thought about things I wanted to do to myself.

My pain and fears turned into pure anger. I fell down next to my bed. I called one of my friends. His name is Derrick. He was an old roommate from my first apartment number 1122. I needed -him to come over really quick. In those moments, I wanted to end everything. I did not want to feel anymore pain. I did not want to fight this battle any more. The enemy had me right where it wanted me. I went to the kitchen to find a knife; I grabbed the first one I could find. I tried to cut myself, but the knife was not sharp enough. I threw the knife and crept into the bathroom hysterically. I knocked over everything as I scrambled for pills. I couldn't find any pills or medicine. I just fell to my knees and started praying. GOD finally had my attention. I began talking to him about everything. I talked to him like never before. I talked to him about my pain, my sorrows, my suffering, and my life. This was the first time I consciously gave all my problems to GOD.

Derrick arrived at the house. I told him everything that happened. My energy was better when he arrived. I told him, "I literally had another mental breakdown". He was a little more familiar with my mental breakdown because he seen me spaz out in the last apartment on numerous occasions. One time my "friends" called me, they told me our television went missing out of the house. I didn't understand how a whole television leave out of a locked house and no one knew about it. So, I spazzed and kicked everybody out. But back to my "suicide" attempt, He was calm and told me he's glad I didn't hurt myself. He told me, "You do anything else crazy; I'm going to have to baker act you." I began to think logically again; I was out on bond and he was politically correct. The last thing I needed was anything else to count against me. I needed to get a grip very soon.

Here's the truth, all of us have made unwise decisions at one point in our life. I'm writing this book to own mines and save lives in the process. There are teenagers, college students, and even adults right now struggling to find themselves. Some struggle with their identity. Some struggle trying to survive in a cold world without guidance. Some have made mistakes. Others are going to make mistakes in the future. They're ambitiously trying to accomplish goals. They're trying to advance to the next levels of life. Many lack support, proper leadership, or positive influences. I'm an advocate for life enhancements, equal opportunities, common practice of equities, and generational foundation stability for those struggling and battling with life obstacles. Our lives matter.

Parents when you send your offspring to school, college, military, etc. please make sure you stay connected with them even if it irritates them. Send them motivational and inspirational messages even if they don't respond. Help them make wise decisions and hold them accountable for their actions at a young age. Show them love and appreciation. Train them to be a leader and allow them to learn from your mistakes. Express to them the power of positive and negative habits. Show them vivid examples for understanding. Don't hide stories from them because you think they cannot handle it. They're young but already exposed to more than you think so, have the uncomfortable conversations early. Educate them on the game of life so the game will not easily get ran on them. Trust is a vital component to any relationship. They will appreciate you later. It could save you time, money, and stress later.

Students and young adults put aside your pride and learn to listen to your wise elders. Most are speaking from experience; they want to see you elevate in life. Please stop being hard headed and stubborn because it usually comes back around to bite you. Stay away from individuals who continues to make bad decisions. If it's family, help them from a distance but don't put yourself in situations that can cost your life or freedom. I've been through it. I don't want you to make some of the same mistakes I've made. Find you a mentor and ask them to help you. You are responsible for your own success, but a mentor helps. Tell them you want to become successful legally. Here's a GEM: *Make sure you surround yourself with positive individuals who will inspire and motivate you to reach your goals.*

My mentor once said, "Show me your friends and I'll show you who you are." I would always debate with him. I would say, "I'm different because I'm doing this and that." But in reality, I was not much different. I was engaged and being influenced by my environment. I'm honest and real enough to admit it. I was not walking by faith. I had the sight of a lost soul.

I had to learn how to use the power of consistency to increase my faith. I was complaining without taking action. I had to reprogram my mind so I can end up where I wanted to be in life. I wanted to elevate. I wanted to be successful. I wanted to be a winner again. I began to learn more about the subconscious mind. The subconscious mind is responsible for most of your habits, positive or negative. I learned it takes only 21 days to break a habit. It takes 21 days to start a habit. Once I understood this concept, I wanted to put it to the test. I had to program direction into my subconscious mind. This concept was similar to The Secret.

Think about this for a second. If you imagine the human body, you will see that everything has a function. Everything functions together to complete only system. Everything aligns and flow in harmony. As I think, my nerves react to help my fingers type each letter to form a word. This book is a collection of thoughts becoming a thing called a book as I stay consistent with the process. I was at a seminar once. A speaker revealed to us that everyone has a business card. The chances of getting a business card reviewed after a conference is not very high. However, a book leaves a lasting impression. A person could really get to understand who you are from your book. A book leaves a legacy. My human body is allowing me to function and leave a legacy. The thought of leaving a legacy is a phenomenon.

I began to develop positive habits. I would listen to books, research and plan. My brother Will told me about a job fair. His job, Xerox, was having a job fair starting out at $10.50 per hour. I was enthusiastic. I was back on the right track and opportunities began to present themselves. I was manifesting victories into my life. My hunger for a heightened level of success increased. I had to kill my ego to embrace this opportunity. I'd previously told myself the "job thing" was not for me. However, I made a sacrifice to accomplish short term goals. In return, I could attain long term goals. I didn't want to get evicted. I didn't want to do something ignorant and disappoint everyone again. I didn't want to fail. I didn't want to give up. I had to stop overthinking so I could put forth action.

I had to identify what really motivated me. Receiving great grades motivated me. Traveling motivated me because it exposed me to more things. My nieces and nephews motivated me to set the bar high so we can break generational curses. My family motivated me with smiles and rewards for accomplishing tasks. Money was a pretty good motivator. Yet, I still had to find internal motivators. I could not always rely on external motivators to turn my gears.

I began to study things around me. I became a student of life. I started by attending the job fair. I dressed up in a suit. I used the suit when I attended forums in School of Business and Industry. We took a typing test and I passed it with flying colors. Florida State University School typing class came in handy. We proceeded to do interviews. I was hired on the spot. They printed my badge and I started the following Monday. Everything happened so fast, I thought it was too good to be true. As I came to work, I studied my coworkers. I studied my trainer and everyone else in the building. It was a relaxed environment. We were getting trained on customer service, inputting information, and policies. The trainer asked about my passions. I told her and said replied, "You should not be here, listen to Rich Dad, Poor Dad by Robert Kiyosaki." I was recommended this book more than once. This time I actually received the message. I was being a true student. I started listening to the book when I got home on Audible.

This book was a GOD sent. I listened to Rich Dad key principles and money lessons. There are many success principles discussed in this book. Rich Dad explained the rich don't work for money; they make their money work for them. This was a new principle and concept. I could not possibly imagine making money work for me when I was struggling to cover my expenses. To understand this concept, I had to dig deeper and pay closer attention. I listened and learned more about cash flows and investments. I found this stimulating and noteworthy because I was taking accounting at the time. I had a D average. Initially, my progression rate was gradual understanding business language. I had to increase my rate of progression on learning brand-new skills, intellectually known as a steep learning curve.

Being honest, I was more focused on gathering the pieces of my life together versus my degree. I remember watching videos of Eric Thomas saying, "You have to want to succeed as bad as you want to breathe." My success was measured in my ability to survive in life. I ended the semester horribly. I fell below the GPA requirements for my scholarships. According to the Satisfactory Academic Progression, I was below the requirement for financial aid too. I was crashing out badly. I decided I was going to take another shot at it. I could not allow myself to fail again.

One morning in training, I was called outside by the managers. I received a bad feeling about this meeting based on the looks on their face. They sat me down at a nice desk and revealed the news. I was a mis-hire. Yes, a complete mis-hire. The trainer was right, I didn't belong there. My background check came back, and I was not eligible for employment there. I gracefully smiled as I turned in my badge. I worked for 3 full weeks to discover I was not going to have the full-time job position. I left and drove to Capital City Bank. I wanted to open a bank account. I saw a classmate name Rob working inside. It was a long line, so I went back to the car. I called my mother and told her the "bad" news. She said, "Well Baby Boy what are you going to do?". I optimistically told her, "Invest!" I feel like GOD sent me on the job site to humbly earn a few hundred dollars and to receive the message from the trainer. I prepared to invest into myself. Additionally, it was time for me to apply for, Spring 2015.

I applied for Spring 2015. I retook the classes from the previous semester. I was more focused and determined to keep my GPA up. After a few weeks of classes, I checked my financial aid. I did not get any financial aid. Furthermore, I had to get a loan to cover the cost of my classes. I was beyond shocked. I went from receiving grants and scholarship to receiving life debt. I thought back to Rich Dad, Poor Dad. The Rich Dad didn't graduate high school, yet he left behind multimillion-dollar businesses. The Poor Dad received his PhD but still struggled and left behind debt. My mind was made up at this point. Entrepreneurship was going to be the way.

I listened to books and wrote down a list of words and phrases along the way. Google became my best friend. I reflected on my list, "Wholesaling, marketing, international trading, seminars, real estate…." I traveled to Atlanta, Georgia frequently for networking purposes. I remember going to Atlanta at a young age. One time my brothers and I went to Atlanta to get some clothes and gold teeth. Montayvious "Humble Tay" Blake, LaDerrion "Lil Dee" Chukes, and I was prepared to stunt on the city. It was Lil Dee 16th birthday. I was only 17 years old, but we got a fancy hotel on a high floor with a nice view. We had the Charger SRT-8 on 24s. We took pictures like we were rich and famous. It was similar to a rap artist tour. This was the first of many trips. I remember taking mental notes of the locations and faces throughout the city.

I stuck out the last semester while taking trips and loading up on merchandise. I wrote down a list of resources I acquired along the way. I began reflecting back on the book, The Alchemist by Paulo Coelho. Santiago was a young Andalusian shepherd boy who desired to travel in search of a treasure. I was searching for a treasure. I didn't know exactly where it would come from or how long it would take to find it, but I knew I was hungry for it.

In search of the treasure and balancing school, life obstacles began to form at home. My mother was experiencing abdominal pains and bleeding. I remember some days I would be on the road and receive pictures that confronted my faith. The doctors began to run test to see if anything was cancerous. The result came back, nothing was cancerous, but she did have to have surgery. I began to worry but she would smile and tell me, "Baby don't worry, GOD will handle it." This fueled me more. I began to grind harder because insurance would not cover the surgery. We didn't have insurance at the time. They would run test and send her home. The next day, she would be right back with the same conditions. I started to feel like Denzel Washington in the movie John Q. But I remembered her words and keep faith in GOD. After enough visits and blood lost, a miracle happened.

A doctor stepped up and said he would do the surgery. This surgery would not cost us any money out of the pocket. My faith increased. Going into surgery our family was at the hospital and my mother was smiling like she had won the lottery. She began to crack jokes to lighten up the mood. I was nervous. I remember sitting in class watching my phone like a text message or call was going to come through with news.

On the other hand, business was doing exceptionally well. I invested my last check from Xerox and started hustling hair, clothes and anything else that could legally be sold. I meet a jeweler and ask them if they could teach me how to make gold. They looked at me like I asked them to build me a house. I guess they didn't think I was serious. My mind said, "Okay, you got your first no so what, keep grinding and stay focused on your mission." I smiled and continue to focus on the business at hand. I remember Les Brown; he went to the radio station many times for a job opportunity as a disc jockey. He heard no multiple times. He did not give up, eventually he was afforded the opportunity to go get a cup of coffee. I was hungry like my mentor Les Brown.

Somehow, I found the energy to remain hungry and keep myself together while keeping faith during the surgery. My mother woke up from the anesthesia. Her vitals were good the doctors said she would have a speedy recovery. This was great news. I proceeded to bring food from BJs Restaurant to the hospital. I wanted to make sure she had some great quality food to eat when she came out of surgery.

Reading Rich Dad, Poor Dad and working the business was actually paying off. On my accounting test, my grades began to increase. I was not studying the homework or book, but the questions became clear. I think this was a result of the management of products and cash. I got my first passing grade on an accounting exam. Prior to working and reading this book, I received a D in accounting. This was a good omen as the wisest man in the world from Alchemist would say. I recognized my ability to connect the dots between real world experiences and book knowledge.

After months of consistently seeing me revisit, my first jeweler stopped me. He asked, "Are you still interested in learning?" Eagerly, I replied, "Yes!" He proceeded to show me a trade that would change my life forever. Aspiring greats are usually humble. I wanted to be great. So, I committed to be a humble apprentice. I started to understand, a student is his own teacher, studying things around him. Studying my environment, I was blessed to find a master who was willing to show me new techniques and skills. Prior to learning, I asked others to teach me, but they did not teach me. One business owner even told me they would help me but when my clients and I arrived at his shop, he tried to take my clients. I was in disbelief. I was so grateful to learn this skill so I could stop trying to work with sharks. Here's a GEM: *Never ask the competition for assistance, do your own research and build your own connections.*

I realized when you really want something GOD and the universe will help you achieve it. I was finally walking by faith. I recall the feelings I received when I got my first set of gold teeth. I was blissful. I was confident. I was courageous. They were like a badge of honor in the neighborhood. Being able to provide this service to our community made me feel like I was making a positive impact legally. I was able to put smiles on faces. Initially, I put one of my cousins in position. Rich Dad, Poor Dad taught me a great formula and I was disciplined. I was learning how to make money work for me while providing opportunities. Besides, I was not confident being in anyone face. I didn't have the best customer service skills. I found a way to delegate as I strengthen my inner self. It was up from there. I was an emerging self-made entrepreneur. At this point, I was not making decisions only for me. It was bigger than me. I was leading by example after my great suffering.

Income increased and I began to celebrate. The boys and I were in the club about thirty strong. Finally, we were able to come back together in good vibes since the death of Chad and incarceration of others. We didn't speak on the past much. It was not the same, but we were "in dat bih" as we would say. We were celebrating collectively, but I went to the club with a different mindset. I was listening to a book called The Power of broke by Daymond John. He is the founder of FUBU and investor on ABC television series Shark Tank. He has humble beginnings and understands what it was like to struggle building businesses in neighborhoods. He knows what it feels like to have nothing to lose. He dropped gems on building a business while being tight on finances.

Listening to his pointers, I began to observe the audience. I had to know my customers, competition, and markets. I had to figure out how I could build brand reputation and get a piece of the show. I continued to vibe in the club and do my homework. I noticed some had on designer clothes, jewelry, and a few had gold teeth. I made a vow that I was going to flood the city and surrounding areas in designer clothes, jewelry, and gold. It was time to speed the city up.

I wanted everyone to have the feeling I felt. I would walk into the club with the hardest outfit, "wet" shining golds, necklaces, and some fresh designer shoes. This was and still is the Florida boy way. I continued to take weekly trips to my distributors and post pictures of the updated inventory. I studied other celebrities while adding my own "sauce" to the equation. I was planting faithful seeds everywhere. I had to believe in the vision of the business, and I did. Everyone else believed in the business too. The entire 850, Tallahassee and surrounding counties area code, supported the movement.

Everyone was watching the process and supporting the business. They would share each post to circulate pictures to boost awareness. This help cut marketing costs. Many people currently ask, "What's the most effective way to market? " My answer is by establishing a well-respected and trusted brand by being honest with integrity. Make sure your products or service is worth every penny. Always give the customer more than what they expect. Build a long-term relationship with each customer, convert them to clients. Here's a GEM: *Word of mouth is the most influential way of marketing*. Each shared post included real testimonies and others loyal clients would tell their friends. I made sure to include my personal story when meeting clients. I had to explain my why. I wanted them to be a part of the mission. Everything was going smooth until another obstacle came roaring into my life.

On April 20, 2015, my mama called me on an early morning after she got hit twice by an 18-wheeler with a gas tank attached to it. She told me she couldn't move and proceeded to tell me she was stuck. As she talked the phone went out. I ran downstairs to my truck. Frantically, I sped out of the gated community and made a sharp right on Tennessee Street. I turned on my emergency lights and busted a right on Mission Road. My mind was made up. If the police got behind me, they were going to have to follow me all the way to the accident. I immediately found myself on Capital Circle passing cars during solid yellow double lanes. I finally made it to Highway 27. I began to drive as fast as I could. I speed through Havana. Everyone from the area know you cannot speed through Havana. One-time Plies, famous Florida artist, tour vehicle got pulled in Havana for speeding. However, I made it to the scene without any accidents or police encounters.

I arrived at the scene. I jumped out of the truck and charged towards the driver of the 18-wheeler saying, "Why you weren't paying attention?" My Auntie Margaret immediately grabbed me to calm me down. She explained to me how GOD had my mother protected and covered. The driver stated he was in the wrong and apologized for the accident. I was not in the right state of mind. My anger was triggered, and I wanted to attack the truck driver. My mother was leaving in the ambulance as I arrived. I glanced at the car. The back of the car was smashed on the gas tank, if it was hit a little harder the car would've exploded. The trailer spun over the car and knocked the door off on the passenger side. I was baffled in disbelief. GOD really had a shield of protection over my mother.

Hours later, she was discharged from the hospital without a scratch. The hospital said last person got into an accident with an 18-wheeler died. People question GOD daily, but I know GOD is real. Here's a GEM: *Stop taking things for granted.* Although my mother was discharged, she was advised not to work. She had to attend physical therapy after attaining internal injuries. The pressure was on more than ever.

I watched my mother work endlessly to get us into a middle-class lifestyle. I was not going to allow us to go below the poverty line. I committed to the hustle. Every single day, I would wake up early to promote, go to class then come sell items until I couldn't anymore. I got on the road with one rapper homies named Kurstin "Chino Fla". We would hit the road together. He saw the vision. Everybody was tuned in with the movement. We were at a distributor when a man had on about 4 necklaces. Chino was like, "Them hard right there." I asked Chino to ask him where he purchased them. The brother told us where we could find them "For da low." This was absolutely perfect. The number one rule to selling products is to buy quality for low and sell it for a higher price. This was the birth of necklaces within the company.

We arrived at the location and I was amazed with the quality for the prices. I purchased six necklaces and charms to test them out. Six had to be a magical number. I put the sets together and posted a picture on Facebook, "Kids chains and charms only $60." The shares and comments did not end. I was sold out within an hour. Reflecting back, this happened five days after the accident. I was walking by faith and not by sight. Sight would have told me to save money for an emergency. Sight would have told me to stick to what I knew best. However, Faith spoke louder. Faith said trust the process. Faith said the business earned the right to grow. Faith said walk with me and I shall exalt you.

Next week, I was catering at my sister Crystal house for a big game. Her co-workers and other family members came to enjoy the high vibrations and mouthwatering food. They poured out great reviews and help me gain more confidence in my cooking business. A few days later, I was heading to Tampa Bay area on faith. My cousin told me he needed me to come down. He said he had some people that needed some jewelry and gold. This was my first time traveling to another major city to provide items. I called Chino and Jamaul Vickers to help assist me along the ride. We were not from the area. Even though it was my cousin, I was still skeptical about going but once again Faith pulled me forward.

I arrived there without a location to set up. I had product, business skills and Faith. We had to make the four-hour drive count. When I arrived, my cousin told me he knew a good spot. True story, we went to a motel and reserved it. We went inside the room and I began visualizing how we could set everything up. Trusting the process, I displayed everything on the dresser and asked my cousin to promote. For the first hour or so nothing happened. Some were not serious and others said they would call back later. Then, we began to have clients call us back to announce they were on their way. We prepared for their arrival and focused on the positive. We had to make sure we left a great first impression.

The first three guys entered. We greeted them like they were walking into a mall store. I said, "Welcome to Delevoe's Lobby" with a bright smile. They browsed our inventory. I began to get to know them and observed which items caught their attention. Growing up, I learned to be very attentive. One asked a question and it was going from there. I asked him, "Would he like to try it on?" He replied, "H*ll yeah!" So, I helped assist him putting on the fine gold set. He got hyped when he looked into the mirror. I saw his friend was looking at exclusive set, so I offered a combo special for both of them. The energy was perfect in the room. The products sold itself. They wanted to get both of the piece and some golds. I went in for the close. We proceeded to make sure they received their packages. We even added gifts for the other friend so everyone could leave with something.

This process was repeated with other customers and we maximized with the limited resources we had available. I'm grateful to have a supportive family, friends and mentors to help assist me along the way. They pushed me to get past the fear of the unknown. The uncertainties of taking a trip with inventory to another city. I remember my dad would tell me stories of how he would travel to different conferences and set up inventory. I realized; I was broke. I did not have hundreds of thousands of dollars in an account. I was just trying to maintain a living. So, I couldn't allow myself to give up before I started. I had to be hungry as Les Brown would say.

I posted a picture on Facebook so they would see we were really grinding, and other cities loved our products. The customers were surprised to see a young black business owner. They really wanted to support because they understood the culture. They understood the struggles. The business was organic. I didn't even realize I was a young black business owner. I was just trying to make a living and provide for my family. I became a source of inspiration in a positive way. This was a new feeling and responsibility.

A few weeks passed and I posted a Facebook status saying, "I always preach you don't have to be a dope boy, crook, or scam artist to have money. I always preach stay humble, work on your brand, and grind hard. I had to grow up and let my old ways go to become a man. They say never let a person know your income. This picture is a statement for my deposits last month $10,568.23. (All Legal) I'm not posting this to boast or stunt. I'm posting this as inspiration for someone to change before it's too late. Living certain lifestyles, it's only two ways out. Don't be a victim. Go to college, get an education and invest into your dreams. The late nights, early mornings are worth it. Don't cheat yourself because the sky is not the limit. Always stay humble and remember there's always room for growth. #HumbleLiving #ThankingGODForProgression #MillionaireBy30 "Amen". Truthfully, I was not counting. I was working and keeping myself busy. I was embracing the process. I started with a map, proof of concept and began to build from the ground up.

My big brother, Tae Tucker, came into to house one day after high school graduation. He saw the jewelry and merchandise displayed on the countertop and kitchen table. He said, "Oh yeah, you got you some right here lil bruh. Keep going, don't stop." I smiled and said, "Thanks bruh, I got you." This meant a lot to me because people really believed in me. The energy I received from everyone, made me go even harder. We went to the club that night for graduation. This was the first time in a while that we hung out together as a group because I was focused on building the business. GOD works in mysterious ways.

A week later, I was on the phone with my dad discussing some business plans when my brother, Will, came up to me. He said, "Bro I think Tae Tae was shot." Initially, I tried to brush it off with a simple, "okay…" I told my dad and opened my Facebook. On Facebook, I began to see others posting statuses, pictures, and even videos. Immediately, I began the grieving process. I was in denial. I thought to myself, "Naw, not Tae Tae… How can somebody shoot

Tae Tae?" He was not the type of person to bother anyone. He was a positive person with great vibes. I reflected back to our last moments. I kept myself strong without allowing my emotions to get the best of me. Well... Partially strong. I did not allow myself to stay locked in a room or away from everything like previous times. I went to his pole to celebrate his life on D-block. Everyone was out there speaking on their memories. Tae Tae is a hood legend. Everybody loved Tae Tae. A voice came to me and said, "Work through your hardest times." So, I paid my respects, showed Northside some real genuine love and started back working. I had to make sure I didn't break down crying on the block. So, I left, worked, and stayed busy for the remainder of the week. I was "all gas no breaks" as we say in Florida.

As his funeral approached, I received a call from Wigg, Mike Larry, about being one of his pallbearers. I was honored but nervous. I tried my best not to allow depression to overtake my life. I remembered what he told me, "Keep going, don't stop." I was going hard the morning of his funeral. I was up early planning. I put on my all white, grabbed my shades and started driving towards the church. I called Will to let him know I was running a little behind schedule. As I talked, I began to hear my voice tremble. I realized; his funeral was really happening. I started praying to GOD as I continued towards the church.

I arrived at the church. It was packed with no parking spaces. I parked down the road and walked up the hill. I entered and had a seat in the front with the rest of the pall bearers. I wore dark shades to cover up my eyes. Everyone spoke on how uplifting his character was when he entered a room. He was not only known in the North-side neighborhood. He was known through communities for being a positive, charismatic uplifting person. He was a leader. As I looked to the right, I saw his mother, Mama Jackie, she held her head high and was covered in the grace of the Lord. The funeral came to an end and we walked him out the church.

Walking him out the church was not a walk in the park. Although it was a short walk, it felt like we walked a few miles. I had hundreds of thousands, of thoughts in those last minutes with him. Last week we were just walking out the club together. Now, we're carrying him outside to a hearse. Even in my positive thinking, I felt the weight of the world on my shoulders. I spoke to Mama Jackie; she gave me encouraging word and much wisdom. I saw where his great energy originated. Here's a GEM: *Appreciate and love the people around you.*

Shortly after his funeral, I received a call about my GODmother, Sharron. She passed away. I could not get a break. She helped potty train me. She would keep me when my mother worked long shifts. We stayed up doing crossword puzzles and putting together 1000+ pieces puzzles. We watched WWE, went to church and even fishing sometimes. Sometimes she would cook pork and beans, rice and fried chicken, one of my childhood favorites. I remember running through Rich Bay, Havana community, all day like Tarzan. She would come out of the house on the front porch, "PJ, come eat!". Now, it was time to say my last Goodbyes.

Her funeral was the following weekend. I posted a status on Facebook, the status reads, "Big bruh last week, GODmother this week. GOD does not make mistakes. I used to get depressed, bottle my emotions, and as a result I was always angry at the world. However, now obstacles in life inspire me to keep going and go harder. I know GOD has a plan so I'm going to continue to trust in him. Y'all stay prayed up and be blessed. Amen." At this point, I could only trust GODGOD's plans. I truly had to walk by faith, not by sight. I had to embody the true essence of faith. I began to use each situation as fuel to inspire me. I could not allow myself to give up based on the things I was experiencing during this part of the journey.

I had a catering event the next day. I prepared and focused on the great moments I shared with everyone who transcended. I changed my perspective. Instead of missing them, I celebrated their life. I started to look at it as a blessing to have shared time with them versus a lost. GOD called them home. I would be selfish to want them here when GOD needs them. Besides, I will make sure they live on in spirit as long as I'm here. This way of thinking generated a sense of peace.

I was on a complete mission. For appreciation, I made sure Quet was loaded with gifts, quality time and great food. She always supported me on this journey. I remember one day I was having a mental breakdown. I called her and said, "I need some inspiration." She sent me a picture; it was hilarious. I could not allow myself to get back mad after opening my messages. My lease for my apartment came to an end. I made a promise to myself. I said, "I will not sign another lease unless it's for a storefront." I started living out of the Infiniti G-37 and my mother's house.

Once I removed the largest debt, luxurious rent, from my life, I was ready to stack up to explore. I did not apply for school the next semester because I was not eligible for financial aid. Additionally, I was not going to take out loans. Resembling the young shepherd in the Alchemist, I was ready to search for my treasure. I began planning for my 21st birthday early. I always celebrated my birthdays. I was finally going to be 21, the legal drinking age. I wanted to experience Las Vegas, Nevada.

I went from being passionate to obsessed. When I started the business, I was passionate. I loved what I was doing. I loved seeing smiling faces. Along the way, after all the experiences, something changed. I still loved what I did but I was obsessed with growing into the best version of myself. I began to see myself in a different light. I began to understand the Law of attraction. I saw the universe would conspire with me. I saw GOD had a great plan for my life. I stopped counting the hours of research, planning, studying, and traveling. I struggled for an entire year, I went to jail, attempted suicide, experienced death of family members, received eviction threats, and subconsciously carried additional weight. But I had faith in GOD. I struggled but I was making progress.

INSPIRATIONAL TRAUMA POEMS

As I Begins — *Poem by Patrice Delevoe*
Created in Honolulu, Hawaii in 2015

As the walls close in, isolation begin
Yowls echo through the room from the door hinge
Hostage captured, the lights run away
Betrayal, dishonestly, overwhelming hate

As the sheets grips tight, suffocation begin
Headphones screeching you're lonely once again
Hostage eyes stare at the wall, such a blank stare
Depression, loneliness, and anxiety feels the air

As the bed cringe, suicidal thoughts begin
Pillows feigned nervously against the cheek
Hostage tears flows, rolling in the deep
Love, trust, respect burglarized without a key

Damaging Promises — *Poem by Patrice Delevoe*
Created in Honolulu, Hawaii in 2015

They say promises are meant to be broken
But a broken heart is never chosen.
The flow of love transition into hate,
Did these promises have to end this way?

Flowing tears, trusting faith
Praying over and over, but slowly fading away
Broken heart, shadowed dreams, empty soul
Promises tearing, every part of me

For better or worse, we vowed to be real
Time and time again, but I can't help but feel
Crushed bruised, naive, and weak
New promises, every day of the week

After a broken heart, one needs therapy
Love, pain, trust, betrayal, honesty!
Each one stripped away, separately
Everlasting damage from promising

INSPIRATIONAL TRAUMA QUOTES

"You will attract everything that you require. If it's money you need you will attract it. If it's people you need, you'll attract it. You've got to pay attention to what you're attracted to, because as you hold images of what you want, you're going to be attracted to things and they're going to be attracted to you. But it literally moves into physical reality with and through you. And it does that by law. (Bob Proctor)" –*Rhonda Byrne, The Secret*

"Life is a cruel teacher. She loves to give you the test first and the lesson later." –*Daymond John*

"When you focus on lack and scarcity and what you don't have, you fuss about it with your family, you discuss it with your friends, you tell your children that you don't have enough - "We don't have enough for that, we can't afford that" - then you'll never be able to afford it, because you begin to attract more of what you don't have. If you want abundance, if you want prosperity, then focus on abundance. Focus on prosperity." –*Lisa Nichols*

"Many people in Western culture are striving for success. They want the great home, they want their business to work, they want all these outer things. But what we found in our research is that having these outer things does not necessarily guarantee what we really want, which is happiness. So we go for these outer things thinking they're going to bring us happiness, but it's backward. You need to go for the inner joy, inner peace, the inner vision first, and then all of the outer things appear. (Marci Shimoff)"
–Rhonda Byrne, The Secret

"Growth is the great separator between those who succeed and those who do not. When I see a person beginning to separate themselves from the pack, it's almost always due to personal growth." *–John C. Maxwell*

"A lot of people feel like they're victims in life, and they'll often point to past events, perhaps growing up with an abusive parent or in a dysfunctional family. Most psychologists believe that about 85 percent of families are dysfunctional, so all of a sudden, you're not so unique. My parents were alcoholics. My dad abused me. My mother divorced him when I was six…I mean, that's almost everybody's story in some form or not. The real question is, what are you going to do now? What do you choose now? Because you can either keep focusing on that, or you can focus on what you want. And when people start focusing on what they want, what they don't want falls away, and what they want expands, and the other part disappears. (Jack Canfield)" *–Rhonda Byrne, The Secret*

"There is nothing noble in being superior to your fellow man; true nobility is being superior to your former self." *–Ernest Hemingway*

"Never give up" *– Cheryl "Mother" Delevoe*

"Turn your wounds into wisdom." *–Oprah Winfrey*

"A friend is someone you share the path with." *–African Proverb*

"I am always saddened by the death of a good person. It is from this sadness that a feeling of gratitude emerges. I feel honored to have known them and blessed that their passing serves as a reminder to me that my time on this beautiful earth is limited and that I should seize the opportunity I have to forgive, share, explore, and love. I can think of no greater way to honor the deceased than to live this way." *–Steve Maraboli*

"We must all suffer from one of two pains: the pain of discipline or the pain of regret. The difference is discipline weighs ounces while regret weighs tons."
–Jim Rohn

"Whether we are speaking of a flower or an oak tree, of an earthworm or a beautiful bird, of an ape or a person, we will do well, I believe, to recognize that life is an active process, not a passive one. Whether the stimulus arises from within or without, whether the environment is favorable or unfavorable, the behaviors of an organism can be counted on to be in the direction of maintaining, enhancing, and reproducing itself. This is the very nature of the process we call life. This tendency is operative at all times. Indeed, only the presence or absence of this total directional process enables us to tell whether a given organism is alive or dead.

The actualizing tendency can, of course, be thwarted or warped, but it cannot be destroyed without destroying the organism. I remember that in my boyhood, the bin in which we stored our winter's supply of potatoes was in the basement, several feet below a small window. The conditions were unfavorable, but the potatoes would begin to sprout—pale white sprouts, so unlike the healthy green shoots they sent up when planted in the soil in the spring. But these sad, spindly sprouts would grow 2 or 3 feet in length as they reached toward the distant light of the window. The sprouts were, in their bizarre, futile growth, a sort of desperate expression of the directional tendency I have been describing. They would never become plants, never mature, never fulfill their real potential. But under the most adverse circumstances, they were striving to become. Life would not give up, even if it could not flourish. In dealing with clients whose lives have been terribly warped, in working with men and women on the back wards of state hospitals, I often think of those potato sprouts. So unfavorable have been the conditions in which these people have developed that their lives often seem abnormal, twisted, scarcely human. Yet, the directional tendency in them can be trusted. The clue to understanding their behavior is that they are striving, in the only ways that they perceive as available to them, to move toward growth, toward becoming. To healthy persons, the results may seem bizarre and futile, but they are life's desperate attempt to become itself. This potent constructive tendency is an underlying basis of the person-centered approach." –*Carl R. Rogers*

"INSPIRATIONAL TRAUMA TO COOPERATIVE TRIUMPH YEAR"

I'M GOING TO BEGIN this chapter with a time lap. I want the reader to see how fast everything can change with the right mindset. The end of December 2014, I landed a job making $10.50 per hour. I was very grateful. My mind was still on a million. Within a year, I was living in Hawaii as a mobile jeweler, creating business plans, and gaining inspiration for a storefront. My mindset shifted from employee to owner. My income increased from $10.50 per hour to over $10,000 per month. Remember, everything can change in one year so don't give up. Warren Buffet, investing guru, confidently said, "The more you learn the more you earn." My 2015 year is living proof of this statement. I took full advantage of Millionaires Mindset Academy resources.

December 2014 – December 2015

Patrice L Delevoe

DECEMBER 2, 2014 ·

Happy Birthday Ko Get Cash Chukes I miss ya... my rider, my shotta, my partner. One locked up, one gone. #RestEasyChad Umma hold it down for yall and I promised yall we gone be straight. The show ain't stopped we still goin... #BowBowBow

DECEMBER 24, 2014 · EDITED ·

I never seen a millionaire sleep. Jay Z makes 96 million dollars per year, but he still has late nights/early mornings because he grind. You have to go hard for what you want without being discouraged. If you're not happy with your finances stop sleeping, stop being lazy and get it by any means necessary. Full time employee and full-time student. You have to want success as bad as you want to breathe. So once again RISE AND GRIND!!!!!

JANUARY 29, 2015 ·

My mama before getting her surgery. She a strong woman, joked and laugh through the entire process. Everything good now and it's finally over. GOD take his strongest soldiers through the toughest battles. She had the family right by her side tho. We done been through worst so we still pushing forward. Everything

MARCH 5, 2015 ·

The wait is over... Next week I'm doing grill all week. Grills will be done before spring break. I'm getting them done on Thursday. I will post new prices later today.

APRIL 10, 2015 · EDITED ·

Happy National Siblings Day to My Brothers, Loyalty Over Royalty. Blood Makes Us Related, Loyalty Make Us Family. Rest Easy Chad #RunningWithTheSameNiggasICameUpWith

#MyHomies #Havana — **with** Andre Whitaker, Will Wiggins, Montay Blake, Dee Miller, Rod Dinero Williams, King Dinero, Mark Cuban, Beaver Mike**and** Real Almightyk.

Patrice L Delevoe is with Cheryl Delevoe.

APRIL 20, 2015 ·

My mama called me this morning right after she got hit twice by an 18-wheeler with a gas tank attached to it. She told me she couldn't move and proceeded to tell me she was stuck. The back of the car was smashed on the gas tank, if it was hit a little harder the car would've exploded. The trailer spun over the car and knocked the door off on the passenger side. Hours later she was discharged from the hospital without a scratch. The hospital said last person got into an accident with an 18-wheeler died. People question GOD daily, but I know GOD is real. Stay prayed up and do not take anything for granted.

APRIL 25, 2015 ·

Kids chains and charms only $60

MAY 2, 2015 ·

We fight party ready!!! Catering by Delevoe's Kitchen

MAY 13, 2015 ·

Brought Delevoe's Lobby To Tampa. Rented A Room Plugged The Hood In With Deals And Back On The Road. Full Time Grinder Pushing 12+ Hours Daily. Numbers Don't Lie Shout Out To Cuh Quay Smith

MAY 30, 2015 ·

I always preach you don't have to be a dope boy, crook, or scam artist to have money. I always preach stay humble, work on your brand, and grind hard. I had to grow up and let my old ways go to become a man. They say never let a person know your income. This picture is a statement for my deposits last month $10,568.23. (All Legal) I'm not posting this to boast or stunt. I'm posting this as inspiration for someone to change before it's too late. Living certain lifestyles it's only two ways out. Don't be a victim. Go to college, get an education and invest into your dreams. The late nights, early mornings are worth it. Don't cheat yourself because sky is not the limit. Always stay humble and remember there's always room for growth.#HumbleLiving #ThankingGOD-ForProgression#MillionaireBy30 "Amen"

JUNE 6, 2015 ·

Last week we were walking in the club this week we're walking big bruh to the hearse. Everything just seen unreal, everybody stay prayed up man#RestEasyTuck

JUNE 13, 2015 ·

Big bruh last week, GODmother this week. GOD does not make mistakes. I use to get depressed, bottle my emotions, and as a result I was always angry at the world. However, now obstacles in life inspire me to keep going and go harder. I know GOD has a plan so I'm going to continue to trust in him. Y'all stay prayed up and be blessed. Amen

JUNE 14, 2015 ·

Delevoe's Catering #Seafood

JULY 2, 2015 ·

Sometimes I Wanna Break Down And Cry, You Don't Know How Bad I Miss You Neva Gone Forget The Times That We Shine. #LiveLongChad#HappyGDayCuh

JULY 29, 2015 ·

Retail Prices $1,799.99
I'm basically giving them away for as low as $600 & $700 with Bluetooth music speakers. Shipping takes no longer than a week. This is the newest and latest innovation on the way that we move. If you're interested or want additional information inbox me.

JULY 30, 2015 ·

When you pull up on her with all her favorites & she acts shy... Happy Birthday Again Baby Quet Renee

AUGUST 9, 2015 ·

Back To School BackPack Special Only $80... First come first serve

AUGUST 13, 2015 ·

When your bundles are really 6A unprocessed & they don't tangle or shed. Inbox me for preorder specials on Delevoe's Bundles

AUGUST 22, 2015 · EDITED ·

When you and your homies do more than just club & party together. #Sophisticated #WeddingDay — with Will Wiggins, Laderrion D. Z. Chukesand Kendra Chukes.

SEPTEMBER 26, 2015 ·

Tears Of Joy – Father remarries

NOVEMBER 1, 2015 ·

Cowabunga #BirthdayWeekend #RitzCarton

NOVEMBER 5, 2015 ·

Baby surprised me, I love her man...

NOVEMBER 7, 2015 NEAR LAS VEGAS, NV ·

I'm country with city boy dreams

NOVEMBER 8, 2015 ·

Delevoe Animation — at Bellagio Las Vegas.

NOVEMBER 8, 2015 ·

Real Snow Bunnies Was Walking Round With Me On The
Strip, Later That Night They Told Me What Happen In Vegas
Stays In Vegas — in Las Vegas Strip.

NOVEMBER 12, 2015 ·

Y'all already know it's my dawg birthday... We suppose to be
turnt right now but I'm over in Hawaii. We turnt up good last
week though & made a real life movie The loyalty we done
built over these years can't really be matched. Right or wrong
we been riding for each other for years. Through the rumors
we done remain loyal... I swear he done got sooooo drunk
so many times I got tired of carrying him in the house and I
just leave him in the car until he wake up in the am. It's crazy
how we done watched each other make mistakes and grow
from them. This my dawg though we done fought some of
each other closes people together and remained real through
it all. Long story short y'all tell my dawg happy birthday and
help him celebrate in Tallahassee for me Love ya Bruh
— with Will Wiggins in Pearl City, Hawaii.

DECEMBER 25, 2015 ·

Merry Christmas from the other side #Hawaii — in Honolulu, Hawaii.

Patrice L Delevoe

DECEMBER 29, 2015 ·

No Regrets Manoa Falls — at Manoa Falls.

4

COLLECTIVE TRIUMPH

THE POWER OF MY STORY PATRICE L. DELEVOE JR.

THE POWER OF MY STORY PATRICE L. DELEVOE JR.

THE POWER OF MY STORY PATRICE L. DELEVOE JR.

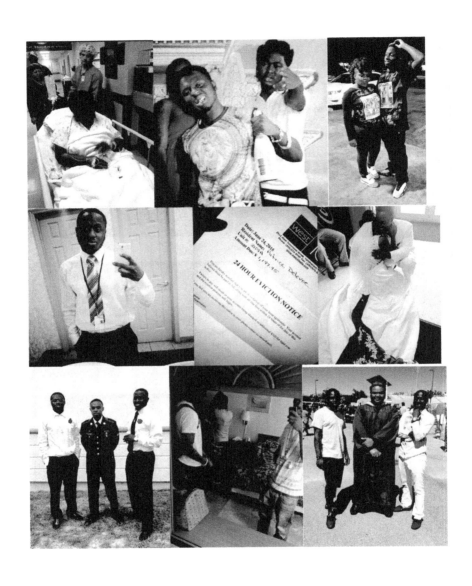

THE POWER OF MY STORY PATRICE L. DELEVOE JR.

THE POWER OF MY STORY PATRICE L. DELEVOE JR.

THE POWER OF MY STORY PATRICE L. DELEVOE JR.

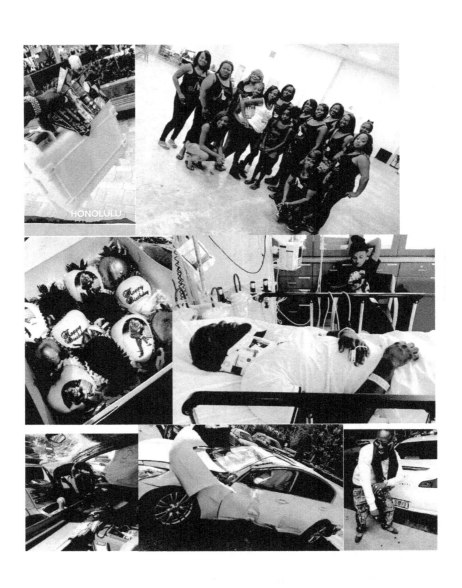

THE POWER OF MY STORY PATRICE L. DELEVOE JR.

THE POWER OF MY STORY PATRICE L. DELEVOE JR.

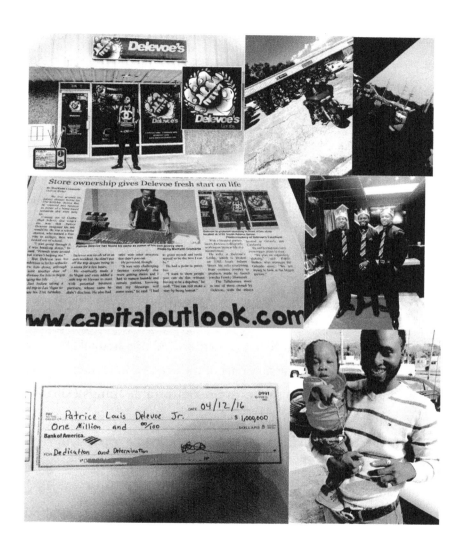

ZIG ZIGLAR FAMOUSLY QUOTED, "What you get by achieving your goals is not as important as what you become by achieving your goals." I wholeheartedly agree with him. The process of becoming a young "successful" entrepreneur positively enhanced me as an individual. I developed more confidence. I grew patience. I learned how to stay focused. I grew integrity. I began to understand the power of networking. I became a risk tasker. I fully embraced my struggles to improve my weaknesses. My dreams, goals, and commitments completely shifted my mindset.

Although great attributes were added to my character, learning has been a painful experience. Here's a GEM: *Block out all the distractions and believe in yourself.* Blocking everything out is not easy. It's easier said than done. When you are familiar with one way of operating, trying a new tactic can cause discomfort. I struggled to allow myself to get uncomfortable. I embraced this struggle because I understood it was a necessary part of the process to form advanced levels of growth. One of the most uncomfortable things I did was pack my bags to leave Florida.

The worse thing in life is regret. As I planned a trip to Las Vegas for my 21st birthday, I noticed flights were much cheaper to go to Honolulu, Hawaii from Las Vegas. My brother and sister lived in Honolulu on the Army base. I told them I was coming to visit but I did not have a date yet. I began to form thoughts. The thoughts began to form a plan. From experience, I knew the business could travel with me. I knew I could set up operations and allow someone to run it. I needed to get out of my comfort zone to take the step. My mission was always to create a business model that could be mobilized. I convinced myself to jump. Thank you, Uncle Steve Harvey, American comedian and spokesperson, for the motivation. I decided to observe the flight prices so I could catch deals. I researched articles online to find the best times to book flights and which airport to departure. Within one week, I booked a one-way flight to Las Vegas, Nevada from Atlanta, Georgia.

The first step of the major transition was complete. I decided to keep my plans a secret. I didn't want to alarm anyone. I decided to stay focus, run the company and support my family and friends. On August 15, 2015, Delevoe's Lobby set up as a vendor at a fashion show by Malik Alrahim in the Moon nightclub. This was a huge opportunity for great exposure and brand recognition. My brothers from another mother, Dee and Montay, was there supporting me alongside one of my fellow classmates James Anderson. We ran to Party City to find items we could use to decorate the vendor table. The theme was black and gold. My first official flyers were complete. Will Wiggins, owner of CDA Designs, made sure our flyers included our inventory and information. A great support system is important starting a small business. There are many unpublicized challenges, but support goes a long way. Without the initial support, I don't know if I could have continued to push forward with the relentless effort, tenacity and drive. The fashion show was phenomenal. We did not make any sales. However, we did gain much needed exposure. Here's a GEM: *Genuine relationships, positive branding, and guerilla marketing are vital keys to growing a business.* I was grateful to have a team who genuinely wanted to see the company grow without asking for anything in return.

The following week, Dee invited William and I to his mother's wedding. Kendra Chukes Bryant, Mama Ken Chukes, was preparing to tie the knot. I had to make sure I was in attendance to serve and witness this beautiful moment. She always went above and beyond to make sure all of us stayed on track. She would buy clothes for some of the brothers with her income tax check. She would give positive advice whether you wanted to hear it or not. She's tough too so don't think everything too sweet. I remember the first time we were arrested as youth. Dee, Greg, Will, Rochon, and I was trying to save the day but ended up going to the juvenile and adult detention facility. I still can't believe them young fellows started with us then pointed us out in a line us with the police officers. I learned to be proactive not reactive. I learned everything does not need a reaction. I learned one wrong move can cost your freedom. I still remember talking about my future handcuffed in the back of the paddy wagon then inside the juvenile center. I thought my life was over.

Mama Ken Chukes came to get the juveniles as soon as she received the call. My mother was working a night shift so she couldn't get there immediately. Mama Ken Chukes was not going to leave us in there though. Greg charges was a little more serious and they would not allow him to leave. This was one of the first time we had to leave a brother behind. This was not a time I could explain or make the problem go away. We were officially considered criminals. Ko Chukes was arrested later that night. Her charges were serious too. I didn't know this was going to be one of the last times we see her. Mama Ken was just helping her fight a previous charge. She didn't want any of us to go down the wrong path. I could hear the word statistic in my head as we got lectured heading back to the vehicles. Somehow, we managed to grow into polished, hardworking, successful young men. We're still waiting for Ko Chukes to come home. I thought about these times as I headed to the chapel.

Will and I arrived at the wedding and helped make sure everything ran smoothly. Our brotherhood was more than partying, fighting, clubbing together. We actively participated in each other's lives like a real brother, blood couldn't make us closer. It was a beautiful experience filled with love and joy. Little did I know; I was about to have another wedding next month. This time it was a little more personal.

My father, Patrice L. Delevoe Sr., called me to ask for my blessings as he remarried. He even wanted me to be his best man. I had two voices, maybe six, speaking to me at once. I will disclose two of them. The first voice, "Sure father, I will support you in anything that truly makes you happy." I was raised to honor my mother and father. The second voice, "Heck no, I'm still traumatized by the divorce of you and my mother." I'm confident he knew my emotions, but he was excited. I didn't want to let him down. I had to be selfless and put my pride to the side, I genuinely wanted to be there for their special day. Gracefully, I accepted his offer and planned to take a trip to Fort Lauderdale.

I was only 20 years old, but somehow, I managed to get a rental car to travel down there. I didn't want to put miles on the Infiniti. I really loved that car. To be completely honest, I didn't go down with a set of expectations. During my growth, I found comfort and peace in most of my traumas. I could not visualize myself as a 20 year old man walking around thinking about what I wish I had as a child. I had to let that pain go. I discovered, it's unhealthy to walk around with resentment in your heart about things you cannot change. So, I decided to be positive. Once again being positive helped me embrace one of my biggest struggles. For so long, I struggled having any type of relationship with my father. I didn't have the capacity to understand why I had to grow up without a mother and father in one household. Subconsciously, I blamed him for other inspirational childhood traumas. But yes, I decided to be fully supportive and there for him on his big day.

I made time to go get fitted for my tuxedo in Tallahassee. I began to realize my dad was really getting married. Inside of Men's Warehouse, the representative excitedly expressed, "Wow, you're the best man." I grinned and finished getting everything prepared. I closed down the mobile shop the weekend. I listened to books and motivational videos as I headed down I-10, I-75, then the turnpike. The road was a peaceful place for me. I could freely think and creatively strategize with minimum distractions. Additionally, traveling through different cities allowed me to gain new perspectives. I was in a peaceful place. I arrived down to Fort Lauderdale. The temperature was pleasant. The energy was great. I pulled into the driveway. I hugged my grandmother and greeted my dad. I arrived right in the middle of preparation.

We headed to the hotel where everyone would gather for practice, food, and other wedding related activities. The scenery was beautiful. We had spectacular views. The outside area was connected to a yacht deck. The water introduced much needed serenity. He introduced me to family and church members, his business friends, and other significant individuals. We drove around like old days preparing. I actually grew a sense of excitement. I was pleased with my decisions to place myself in an uncomfortable environment.

We practiced coordination and so forth. As the bridesmaids and groomsmen gathered, one of my dad's multimillionaire friends, Mr. Craig Sweet, showed me many things about character. He explained to me, the loudest in the room usually have the least to offer. He told me to focus on passive income, he discussed the international travel company. I remember glancing at his Yacht Master watch as he talked. It was not even gold; it had a gray hue. I watched one of my "cool" cousins get drunk, brag about his possessions, and pick arguments. The bridesmaids were not impressed. However, they found the quiet groomsmen more attractive. Everyone there had businesses, valuable possessions, and status in their industry. However, they were not boasting it. This increased my value for humbleness.

I didn't have a million dollar business yet. I had no room to beg or boast about wealth. I was not truly wealthy. Most wealthy individuals do not ignorantly flaunt their wealth. Additionally, I listened to conversations. They spoke on values, ethics, and many positive experiences. My cousin, Ed, talked to me about the car dealing business. My cousin, Todd, joked about some life experiences. Alongside, his diligent work as a black licensed contractor for skyscrapers. We glimpsed outside as he explained how many stories his license allowed him to contract. His friend, Earl, a prestigious surgical doctor, found interest in my passions and ambitions. I went to talk to my dad. He was enjoying the moments.

I felt like I was in a movie. He was outside the door of his future wife. They were talking. He could not see her. This was a tradition. The groom is not supposed to see the bribe before the actual wedding. My perspectives begin to change. He had all these great people here, but he wanted me to be his best man. I began to feel less resentment and embraced the emotions attached to honor. I went back to my room and talked to my cousins, Mari and his friend. Mari was committed to football. I listened to him talk about his passion. I shared a few stories with them about my business ventures, childhood, and passions. They were actually interested. They found inspiration a sense of inspiration from it. The night ended.

We woke up the next morning and prepared for the wedding. The wedding was held at Reverend Samuel Delevoe Memorial Park. We rushed there to prepare everything. We set up the tables, chairs, and decorations. I watched my dad friends step in to do things to lighten the load. I aimed to keep my dad anxiety under control, he was doing so much at once. I saw myself in him. It was like the future version of myself.

The wedding started. Our families gathered in harmony. During the exchange of vows, my Dad started singing. You could hear the passion in his voice. Phelicity, bride, started crying and everyone broke into tears. I couldn't believe I had thoughts of missing it. This was a beautiful moment. As I held the rings, I began to see how the importance of the role. My uncle, Pastor Sam, solemnized the marriage. Prior to 2015, I never attended a wedding. I only watched them in movies. We walked around the park to take some professional pictures. I was able to grow and develop so much from the experiences. I formed a greater sense of gratitude for our relationship. Thankfully, I had to get back on the road to prepare for my birthday.

As I headed back to north Florida, I developed relationships with sponsors and future partners. Randomly, I had a blowout. I began to laugh because I had to get out of the car while it was raining cats and dogs to change the tire. The trucks wind blew fiercely shaking the car as I lifted the jack. I had to move expeditiously. I could not allow anything to steal the experienced joy away from me. This is just an example of how life will happen to you in the process of receiving blessings. I could have reacted differently, but I saw it as a part of my testimony. So, I did not act out of emotions. I focused on the blessings versus the mishaps.

I jumped right back into grind mode. The city missed me while I was gone. I was able to run the businesses in my brother Dee apartment for a couple of months to build capital. This apartment had become a trap. We were taking risk to achieve profits. Homecoming was approaching so everyone grind was in full effect. I remember seeing Bobby Fishscale and Youngin YK swerve through with I.S.N stamped on the side of their cars. Everybody was focused on running up a check and building a brand. During this time, our area was going through a molly epidemic. The once loved party drug had begun to spread through communities like wildfire. They classified this molly as "Flokka". The area just got hit with it out of nowhere. Here's a GEM: *Never do business where you lay your head.* One of our closest brothers broke into the house and stole a hoverboard, Xbox one, and other valuables. It seems like every time we tried to take steps forward, we would take losses to get knocked a few steps back.

This helped me understand the power of drugs in a community. Drug overpowered the same individuals we fought, played, fellowshipped alongside. It became common to see somebody pull out a "woo" blunt, little tobacco and molly, to smoke right in front of you. It became a drug of choice. My advice to anyone reading this book would be to stay far away from drugs. If first, you started doing the drug but eventually the drug start doing you. Don't allow yourself to build the habits of depending on drugs as a way to escape your "reality". Don't allow peer pressure to guilt trip you into trying substances you would not try by yourself. Be a leader, we need you. My mother was always a great leader in this area. She does not drink or smoke. She reminds me frequently.

On a mission to lead and inspire, it was time to enhance the vision. This mission could not be achieved locally. It was time to spread my wings like an eagle. On a journey toward my personal legend, I had to prepare for the big move. I knew I could only learn so much in Tallahassee. Additionally, I wanted a fresh start with new opportunities and less distractions. I loved everybody but I needed some time to myself to gain clarity, peace, serenity, and organization. This led me to book a one-way flight to Honolulu, Hawaii from Las Vegas, Nevada. My family told me I could come live with them until I had everything figured out. They told me, "You straight, you don't have nothing to worry about." I love and respect them so much for affording me this opportunity. I was not in school. I was a full-time student of life. I had a dream and a few dollars. In other words, I was pursuing my personal legend, my treasure.

As I prepared, I made a public service announcement on Facebook. On November 2, 2015 I announced, "Dear Facebook family and friends, my birthday is approaching in two days. This will be my last big celebration of this year in Tallahassee. I'm leaving this Thursday heading to Las Vegas then moving to Hawaii. My website will be up for all of my customers to purchase items from Delevoe's Lobby. I will have someone here handling packages for grills. Come out and turn up with me for my birthday @ the Moon... They wanted me to have a birthday bash in Atlanta but I'm going to turn up with the 850 one last time before I go... I will post more information about my 21st YRN invite only pregame strip party before the moon. #Like #Share #Support #ItsBeenGood850". I got many comments, likes and shares. Some individuals were sad because I was leaving while others congratulated me for continuing to progress.

This next precious lesson could possibly save your life. Here's a GEM: *Do NOT drive fast in the rain or drink before driving.* I thought it would be a phenomenal idea to bring in my birthday with my cousin, BK, during a rainy night at el patron. His birthday was a day before mines. The next day I updated my status with picture of the Infiniti stating, "On our birthday last night my cousin and I was involved into a horrible car accident. Avoiding a collision with another car, I turned, lost control and stuck two steel poles that resulted in the car hanging off a 12 foot cliff. The steel pole was inches away from going through my head. If the airbags would not have deployed, we could've been killed on impact. Everyone was scared to look in the car. People question GOD daily, but we made it out of this car without a scratch only soreness and pains. Material stuff can be replaced but GOD spared our lives. Amen." I remember getting pulled out the passenger side of the car, there was smoke, and you could smell the fluids from the engine. There were two ambulance, one for me and one for BK. Many witnesses were outside of the vehicle nervously watching and on their phones. I walked into the ambulance, the paramedic began to talk to me, and I passed out. I remember waking up in a room with my mother and Dee Chukes. I felt like a new person. I know this is going to sound irrational. However, I believe this was a rebirth or reincarnation. My life changed.

After surviving the accident, I had to get my phone repaired because it shattered in pieces. It was in my left pocket. The impact from the collision bent the phone and shattered the glass. Nevertheless, I was determined to continue my 21st celebration. I already had two special dancers, a personalized birthday cake, room reservations, and sent invitations. I did not want to cancel due to any circumstances. So, I proceeded. My mother took me to go look at the car. Tears came from her eyes when she saw the damage. I think I was still in shock. I just looked at the Infiniti, took pictures then grabbed a few items from the inside. All my jewelry, money and other valuables was inside the glove compartment. I didn't want any of the staff or officers to think I was a drug dealer. I didn't want to be stereotyped. As we drove off, I tried my best not to ponder on it. She always explained material things can be replaced but my life cannot. To be completely honest, I was embarrassed. I feel like I was letting her down once again.

I tried my best not to show it. She dropped me off to Hotel Duval. I checked in and prepared for the celebration. I made sure I had everything we needed for a YRN, Young Rich N****, party. I was being very impulsive. I was spending money and making money. Derrick and Will brought me some salmon, potatoes, and broccoli from Logan's Restaurant. They joked and called me "Boujee". I was preparing for everything, but I didn't even eat prior to them bringing me a birthday dinner. They knew how I was when I'm fully engaged on getting something done. They helped me run the last errands. I am so grateful for them.

The room began to look like a party. The bar was set up with top shelf. Sineaktra Atkins finished my last-minute request for my boss cake. The cake had a money bag, a necklace, an iPhone, and a stack of money. I felt like I was the legit hustler of the year. The music was getting set up. The entertainers were on their way. Finally, I changed into my birthday fit. I pulled out the all Gold Robin Jean Jacket with the Balmain Jeans. I had to find some last minute one-dollar bills. Will told me he had a surprise for me. He walked me down to the lobby area and a camera came out of nowhere. It was Tally TV. I would do all these things without having any documentation. He shocked me with this one. It was really about to be a movie.

We walked back up the stairs, I said a few things for the camera then we entered the room. The party began. Without disclosing too many details, I would simply say the pregame was a success. Every selected guest enjoyed themselves, entertainers were paid, and we were on our way to the Moon nightclub. We arrived at the club for about an hour before it ended. We hit the dance floor and partied for the remainder of the night. This was the perfect 21st celebration in town. Now, it was time to prepare for my flight. Well that was the plan.

I went back to the hotel for some rest. I spent some of my last moments conversing with my partner. We held each other and romanced like a love scene in the 90s. I woke up late the next morning. My mother came to get me, and we headed home. I quickly packed my clothes. We expeditiously hit the interstate and proceeded to head to Atlanta, Georgia. As we drove, I watched the time and noticed I ran the possibilities of missing my flight. I began to look at other flight prices. They were outrageous due to a last minute booking. I began to gain a sense of doubt. I thought to myself, "GOD will not bring you this far to drop you." As we traveled down the interstate, I began to think about my last 48 hours. I was passed out unconscious after experiencing a near death experience, celebrated 21 years of life, now heading to Atlanta to move thousands of miles away. I didn't have a car anymore. I went over my budget for my birthday celebration. But I had a room booked in Vegas for one of the 3 nights. I also had a flight to Honolulu, Hawaii. I could not allow any circumstances to turn me back now. I continued to have faith.

Finally, we arrived at the airport terminal. I rushed out of the car with my bags. I hugged my mother, shook Bobby hand and kissed and hugged Quet Renee. I grabbed and ate another strawberry with our picture on it. She surprised me with that alongside other gifts for my birthday. Also, I made sure to take the bible with a handwritten message from her, "We've been through a lot already, and have many more hurdles to cross, but I can't wait to cross them together. I pray that our love for each other will flow more and more. And, that we will keep growing in our knowledge and understanding." I took this with me to keep me grounded. I always tried to do right but sometimes I would drift into the world.

I arrived at the front counter. They told me, "You are too late for your check in bags." My flight was nonrefundable. I had no choice but to book another flight or go back home. I checked my bank account and booked another flight. I checked in bags and paid additional fees for bags. I went back outside to spend some time with my family. I told them what happened and left supplies with my mother to sell. I was going to keep them, but I had to sell them for additional funds. I made sure I went back inside the airport on time to check in. This was the first time I would be traveling over 500 miles independently.

Positive affirmations constantly reminded me, "I am chasing my dreams. I am living my life with purpose on purpose. I can, I will, I must. You have to be hungry. Your personal legend awaits you." I got pass security and boarded the plane. I looked down at my ticket. It read Las Vegas, Nevada. I thought to myself, "Not bad for a country boy." I always had city boy dreams. I sleep most of the flight. I thought the highways was peaceful until I flew thousands of feet in the sky.

I had a delay in New York City. Then, I flew towards Las Vegas. I remember glancing out the window. I saw the Rocky Mountain. I thought things like that only exist in history books. I believe I have always been skeptical about things. I landed in Las Vegas. Stepping into the airport, slot machines were everywhere. My eyes grew big as I walked through the airport. I went to baggage claim, picked up my bags, and headed to the pickup area. At this moment reality hit, I only had a few dollars in my account. Literally a few dollars. I used the dollars I had to catch a taxi downtown. The scenery was amazing.

I was not completely worried about financial challenges. I appreciated the views. I appreciated the freedom. I appreciated the treasures of the universe. I arrived downtown. I got dropped off at The Palazzo. Initially, I was going to stay there but life happened. I walk through the lobby. I paid close attention to the architectural works. I could feel the upscale, luxurious lifestyle in the atmosphere. I looked into my contacts and reached out to a few partners. I learned to always keep a few contacts that you could reach out to in a time of need. Additionally, I had merchandise to sell. I didn't worry or stress. After an hour or so, I began to get tired of carrying the bags. My phone was going dead from the social media apps and nobody contacted me back yet. The sell did not go through with my mother yet. So, I was stuck without a room for the first night. By the grace of GOD, Earl, my mentor and partner contacted me and told me he was doing surgery. He was heading to send me some money for my birthday and Las Vegas.

I was raised to be independent. I lived on the principle that one man not supposed to ask another for anything. However, I grew to realize wealthy friend focus more on impact, meaningful relationship, potential business opportunities, value and so forth. They do not mind helping friends in a time of need as long as the friend does not try to take advantage of them. The things that were big to me were small to some of them. I explored until I found a Western Union. I made a deposit into the ATM and booked the nicest room for the best rate. The signature at MGM Grand had a reservation with my name on it.

Arriving to the front, valet open the door and I allowed concierge to get my bags. I went to the front desk to check in. I requested a high floor room with the best view. I received the keys to my room. I got in the elevator and clicked floor number 30. I walked down the hallway, entered the room and stood there for a few minutes. I was living in the moment. I was not stuck depressed in my past or dreaming into my future. I was living in the current moment. I was in Vegas. I was 30 floors up with a remarkable view. I stepped out onto the balcony and yelled. It was better than I envisioned. I was thankful and grateful for life itself. I couldn't believe I wanted to end it all a year earlier.

I search for the television. I saw the remote but no television. I pressed the power button and it came out of the desk. The 42 -inch flat screen came out of the desk. I went into the bathroom. The floors were marble, and the tub had jets. I was so tired from the accident, party, road trip, and flight. I literally took a bath with the jets on. It was so relaxing. I cut on some music, increased my vibrations and embraced the serenity. I finished my therapeutic bath, revisit the balcony, prayed to GOD, and went to sleep.

When I woke up and checked my checking account. It had almost $300. I called my mother and to see if she deposits any money. She told me she was in line to deposit it now. The sell was delayed but not denied. I said thank you and hung up the phone. I checked again and began thanking GOD for working everything out. I still do not know where the extra money came from. Moments later, my mother deposit the sell from the items into the account. I kept faith. I trusted the process. I was disciplined. Now, I was able to enjoy my 21st birthday in Las Vegas. I was even able to extend my day for another day for a discounted rate. I learn how merchandise is more valuable than loose cash because while in Vegas enjoying myself, the company was able to sell a few necklaces and bracelets.

I ordered breakfast in bed, got dressed then explored downtown. I networked, meet individuals who were young and ambitious. The energy was extremely welcoming. We discussed what it was like chasing dreams. We came to an understanding that obstacles are only there to test your faith. When you are truly chasing your dreams, you will receive both positive and negative signs. We were able to bless each other with high vibrations. It was relieving to know I was not just some crazy, delusional person chasing a dream. I was not the only person risking everything. I enjoyed crossing paths with like-minded passionate, ambitious individuals. Later, I reserved a room at Caesar's Palace. The movie Hangover was filmed there. I knew it would be a great experience.

I checked in and looked out the window at the courtyard. I was not 30 floors up, but the view was incredible. I felt like I was in a castle. I dived into bed. For some reason, I enjoyed the peace of being in the room alone. My brain was able to think without influences. I treated myself to Bacchanal Buffet. It was ranked the number one Las Vegas buffet by USA Today. I loaded my plate with snow crabs, steak, shrimp, and any other appetizing food that caught my attention at the bars. I tasted a chain of desserts and ice creams. I was like a kid running around in an unlimited candy shop.

Sitting with a stuffed stomach, I reflected on a couple days prior. I didn't know how I was going to eat. I didn't know where I was going to sleep. I just knew I couldn't sleep on the dream of experiencing Vegas on my 21st birthday. But now I'm eating dinner in one of the top-rated hotels in Vegas. I was receiving GOD's grace. I was at the table in my white Gucci Foamposite, all white Gucci tracksuit, wearing ten gold rings like Mansa Musa of Mali. I confidently posted videos on Snapchat and Instagram to show my follower to chase their dreams without doubt or fears.

The last night was spent downtown. I reserved a room at the Golden Nugget. I walked the strip all night. A group of young men were freestyling. One of the artists started his flow on The Notorious B.I.G, he came in saying, "I came to sin city with a dream, working hard every day, it's reality, I'm running in a race and I'm on a full battery..." I smiled and continued to enjoy the Fremont Street Experience.

I arrived back to the room. I began to gain excitement for Honolulu, Hawaii. It had been a while since I saw my brother, sister, nieces, and nephews. Besides, I experienced everything on my list plus more. My passion for traveling for increased during these moments. I was ready to explore the possibilities in Hawaii. I began to Google different attraction. I created a budget list.

Leaving Vegas heading to Hawaii, I was amazed at how far faith and determination could take a person. Initially, I only had a few dollars and a dream. The dream was enough to propel me forward. I took action towards my dream. GOD blessed me with many gifts and visions. I didn't have everything figured out. Rationally, it did not make sense. But GOD, my strong belief system, and philosophies allowed me to take the risk. I was landing in Hawaii. A young country kid from the projects and a small town was landing in Hawaii with a traveling business. This was beyond me.

Once I arrived, my big brother gave me a tour of the island. We entered through the gates of the Army base and arrived at the two-story house. My nieces and nephews ran up to me. I surprised them by coming into town. I felt like myself again. Away from all forms of distraction, surrounded by love, focused on the task at hand. I entered the Millionaires Mindset Academy. I downloaded more books and studied uncompromisingly. I was hungry for knowledge, formulas, wisdom, and understanding. One early morning, I stepped on a scale. I noticed my weight was twenty pounds heavier. I was eating big boy meals without thinking about my model body. I took off my shirt and I had man boobs. I was not confident with my appearance. At this moment, another transition began.

I learned to be discipline instead of going out partying and clubbing. I locked myself in the room to listen to books and documentary videos while taking as many notes as I could. I found Dr. Sebi. I had to be intentional. I could not allow myself to settle. I received knowledge about unhealthy foods such as pork, red meats, and artificial drinks. How could I love myself if I was physically poisoning myself? How could I live a long life without disease? I needed to make adjustments and fast. Immediately, I began to jog in the mornings and ate only healthy foods. I had a clear vision. Like before, faith was going to make my vision a reality. I worked and saved. I made sure my shipments were still coming to both Hawaii and Tallahassee. My partners Will and Hakim help run Delevoe's Lobby while I was away, and I worked Delevoe's Lobby in Hawaii. I would travel downtown to the Ala Moana Center. Ala Moana is the ninth largest shopping mall in the United States and the largest open-air shopping center in the world.

This was a perfect opportunity to network with high end clients and seek inspiration for the future store. I dressed up with my brother Invicta collection box and browsed the mall. I entered high end stores like Rolex, Gucci, CHANEL, Louis Vuitton, and many more. I observed their customer service, elegant displays, and luxury goods. Each company represented a luxury brand. This sparked ideas, set tones and inspired a vision. I actually didn't make any sales on this day. Nevertheless, the experience was valuable in-it-self.

After months of learning and exploration, it was time for me to survey California and meet with potential business partners. I put most of my resources into this trip. I took another calculated risk. I gambled meeting with many other partners to meet with one business partner in particular. Nevertheless, this partner was strongly considered due to their relentless efforts, drive, ambition, and organization. I had good faith; I was confident it was going to be worth it. I prayed and asked GOD to lead me in the right direction. I knew I had the power to manifest it. Whatever "it" was.

Upon arrival, I called my potential business partner but did not receive an answer. I proceeded to catch a bus from the airport to the rental car center. My departing flight didn't leave for the next four days. I had to figure it out. If this business meeting did not go through, I was going to live in the car and networking every single day. This was the first time attempting to get a rental car in my name. I was not sure if I could get it because I did not have a credit card. I only had a debit card. I was able to get it because I had a departing flight. I proceeded to pick out a car from the rental terminal. I saw a cool Hyundai. I pointed to it, received the keys, and drove outside of the gates. I felt like I was on GTA. I turned on the radio station, turned up the volume to the limit and blasted "California Love" by 2pac and Dr. Dre. My vibrations increased as I drove through the streets of LA looking at the scenery.

I was on the west side. I completely lost track of time. The street lights were on before I realized it. I don't know if it was because I was enjoying driving up the hills looking at mansions, getting blown off the road for recording clips to show my followers or simply because I was living life to the fullest. It was perfect timing because my phone alerted; it was time to meet. There was nothing to worry or stress about when my potential business partner did not answer or return my calls. He was traveling back to town from another business meeting. I learned a valuable lesson. *Make the best of any situation.* I could've sat in one place worrying, complaining, lacking faith but I took action. I explored areas and squeezed in time for a nice unhealthy burger.

I went to In-N-Out Burger to check them out. I was told they had the best burger in the area. They were near the airport too, so I gave them a shoot. I got my fries load with their sauce. If you ever been to In-N-Out Burger, you know it's necessary to get the sauce. By the time I got finished consuming the great unhealthy burger, my future business partner arrived. He hopped out and we greeted each other. I proceeded to follow them to his house.

We traveled to a remote location. I was skeptical at first. Imagine driving for hours behind a car of individuals with dreams and faith. Imagine being by yourself thousands of miles from your closest family, friends, and loved ones. This was definitely by faith not sight. I was not focused on immediate financial gains or gratification. I needed to connect with someone who saw my vision. I needed someone who could think big with me. We arrived at the house.

I was amazed. He relocated and created an empire. I was inspired by his ability to build a business from the ground up. We discussed a few business plans. He gave me some pointers and tips to help me get organized. Organization helped me gain clarity. I discussed my food business. We went to the store and grabbed some items for the house. I took advantage of the opportunity to cater dinner for the evening. I enjoyed cooking on the gas range stoves. Fire flamed up as I mixed sauces. It was an iron chef experience. I received phenomenal reviews. I have always been passionate about my food business. However, I presented my second love, jewelry.

He asked me questions like, "Where you want to open it?", "How big you want it cousin?", "What's the inside going to look like…?" These questions begin to catch me by surprise. I was supposed to have the answer to these questions. I stumbled upon a GEM: *Make sure you have a solid plan.* A plan you know is going to work based on calculations. A plan you actually scaled, measured, and tested. I didn't have the answer to some of the questions, but I had Google. I began to research store fronts. I visualized the size of my apartment. I gathered data of my resources. I calculate profits from each product sold to set a quota for daily sells. I broke the numbers down so I could see the dream was possible. When I was going to college, I was aiming to earn at least six figures per year. I scaled the business to make at least six figures.

I reflected back to the luxury stores in Hawaii. The luxurious experience included outstanding customer service, welcoming smiles, aesthetically pleasing décor, and so forth. My mission was to make our customers ongoing clients. I planned to celebrate with our clients as they accomplished milestones in their life. Delevoe's Lobby was going to be more than jewelry hustlers. We were in the making of creating jewelry family.

Within a few days, I had three prospect location, layout designs, startup cost, estimates for the year, policies, positions, and miscellaneous information. I was finally organized. Every other hour, he would enter the room and hype me up. The energy alone helped me believe in myself more. I knew I was capable of great accomplishments. However, after many failed attempts, struggles, and adversity sometimes I would beat myself up. Here's another GEM: *Be the energy you would like to receive.* Watching him successful run his business while pushing me to organize, strive, and accomplish my dreams fully embody this principle. We discussed a few more things and I was on my way back to the airport.

I contacted Will to come get me. He was one of the few that knew I was coming back to town. It was not a secret, but the public announcement was not prepared yet. He drove his Impala all the way to Atlanta to get me. He called her Betsey; he drove Betsey all the way to Atlanta. If you were in our circle you would understand why this was big. I'm laughing as I am writing. Betsey made it up there too. Arriving in Atlanta, I checked my bank account and began to get shipments overnighted, so I'll have merchandise when I arrive back to Tallahassee. I didn't tell anyone any of my plans. When I got back, I set up a reservation to get a car. I arrived at Enterprise and received bad news. I was not able to rent a car and they did not have any cars available. I did not take this answer as a no. I took it as a delay. This was another part of the puzzle I had to figure out. I stood up there trying to figure out a strategy. But Will had to work.

During this time, he was working at Zaxby. My cousin/brother Trevor Chambers, rich homie, was in the area at the time. He was with a young lady. She was twenty-one years old. I asked her if she would rent me a car for me to run a business. She agreed. We went back to the rental car lot. Everything was going smooth. I went outside to talk to Trevor. We were talking about some of the old days. Trevor always had positive energy. He would come up with a bright smile and hug you like a polar bear. She came outside, she said she was not able to get the car because she didn't have a light bill. I walked back in. I could not take no for an answer.

Five minutes before closing, the manager asked me to come to the counter. She told me, "You have been here all day." She saw my persistence. I explained to her, "I have a business." She told me she could not find it. I had a "business", but it was not incorporated with the state. So officially, I didn't have a business. By the grace of GOD,

I ended up with some keys at a discounted rate. I even upgraded to an SUV. It was beyond my understanding. I heard a voice in my head, *Lean not on your own understanding.* I told Trevor and his friend thank you. I drove back to Will job, grabbed a few bags out of Betsey, and proceeded to run the business.

The next business day the rental car from California posted and my account went to negative -$289. How did I allow that to happen? I went from a dollar and a dream to products and a plan. I would work to 3 am in the morning sleep in the truck and start back working at 7 am. I was dedicated to open a store. I drove to each location. I was in favor in the location on Adams Street. This location was centralized. The students could walk from Florida A & M University if necessary. The price was affordable. At this point, I just had to take the first step.

I made the phone call. I set up an appointment with the realtors. We would've converse differently if they would have known I was sleeping in an SUV in front of their property. Optimistically, I scheduled the meeting as soon as possible. I did not want to lose momentum. It's very important to continue capitalizing when you have momentum. Here's a GEM: *Ride your wave until you cannot ride it anymore.* I meet with her the following day. She was very nice as she gave me a tour of the unit. I drew a layout as I walked inside of the building. I claimed it. I called one of my business partners, bossed up client, to reveal the plan. For the most part, he already knew. He was waiting on me to give him a call. I pulled up on him to meet. He asked me a few questions. I had an answer and calculation plan for every question. Remember this quote, "*Preparation plus opportunity equals success."* Within twenty-four hours, GOD sent my Angel investors, Jamie & Cousin, to place the deposit money directly in my hands. I made a phone call to my mother. I told her I was going to open a store.

On January 26, 2016, I posted a status on Facebook stating, "I just want to give a special thanks to everybody that has supported me. It has not been easy starting and building a business from the ground up. However, GOD has allowed me to open my first store. Hard work does not go unnoticed. I promise I won't let my family, supporters, or people watching me down. Delevoe's Lobby grand opening coming soon. #BusinessOwner #YoungBoss #DelevoesLobby #HumbleBeginnings #Like #Share #Support" My supporters helped me celebrate this moment and spread the word around.

I was prepared to build a store on faith. My Angel investors granted me a percentage of the startup funding to get started. To be completely honest, I was not expecting it. I grew to live by the motto: *No expectations, no disappointments.* I was hustling relentlessly every single day. I was sleeping outside and waking up daily to make it happen. I became determined to manifest this plan. But I was not the only one. My Angel investors make sure EVERYBODY EATS. GOD sent miracle workers and funds helped get the ball rolling. It was deeper than the funds for me. I saw someone taking a part of their hard earned money to invest into my dream. I saw someone taking the time out of their busy day to motivate me. I saw someone who wholehearted believed in me. Sometimes all a person needs is the right energy. Here's a GEM: *Make sure everyone around you want to see you win.*

Coming from the neighborhood projects, I had to fight for everything. I had to fight for respect. I had to fight to keep my nice things. I had to fight against my struggles. I had to fight my emotions. I had to fight mentally and physically. I had to fight for my manhood. My Angel investors, who developed into my brothers, showed me I was not fighting alone. Their mission was to help Delevoe's Lobby get on autopilot. They wanted to see Delevoe's Lobby in a winning position. I remember having a big brother, little brother conversation with my brother, Way. He told me he didn't want anything to happen to me out here in these streets. I love and respect the guidance, leadership, and brotherhood. I was grinding all day every day. I was focused on the positive, but I couldn't ignore the fact that two Tallahassee entrepreneurs experienced tragedies a year before due to homicides. I send my condolences to the family of Aaron GODwin, founder of Exclusive Heat, and the CD man. Both of you will forever be legends in the community. I realized every community has a Nipsey Hussle. I was inspired by their hustle, grind, and tenacity.

One of my investors introduced our marketing specialist, EMG Designs. EMG measured our windows for the storefront signage. He provided us with promotional posters, eye catching flyers, and additional marketing material. I was new at most of these tasks, so he helped me save money while providing top quality. Step-by-step, piece-by-piece, everything was manifesting. GOD was blessing the business and aligning it all together. It was not forced, it was flowing.

I learned to form phenomenal business relationships with professionals. They help establish your business. I learn to form phenomenal business relationships with clients. They help build your business. I learned to form phenomenal relationships with your team. They help operate your business. When you form the right relationships with the right individuals, life becomes less challenging. It takes a village.

As I worked towards the vision, the rest began to align. I began to receive job applications before I typed an application. I began to do interviews before I know which questions to ask. I began to receive help without asking for help. Everyone wanted to see me win. They believed in me. Everything began to move so quickly. Within a few weeks, Bobby, father figure growing up, built a wall with a window to form an office. The window allowed me to see sales floor from the inside of the office.

My Uncle Melvin and Ricky quickly installed the floors. We were on a time crunch. Neighbors were moving into the unit next to us. We were using the unit as a storage, but we had to pick up the pace. I walked into the store to see the painter working on the roof while Uncle Melvin and Ricky were knocked out the floors. I would stand to observe. We moved half of the furniture inside the store. We had a huge check-out counter from a department store in Atlanta. The check-out counter would not fix through the doors, so we left it outside. I set it up and used it until we were able to put it inside the store. The windows on the outside were tinted.

I ordered two chandeliers. I was inspired by the luxury designer stores in Honolulu, Hawaii. I wanted Tallahassee, surrounding areas, and travelers to receive the same feeling when they enter. Our contractor, Derrick Gamble, installed the chandeliers. Mr. Gamble really helped many of Delevoe's Lobby visions come to life. He would brainstorm with me. We would look through picture than make it come to life. He always came and finished the job. He cut the desk in half and rolled it inside. He glued it back together, painted it, and smiled. The desk looked better than before. It didn't look like it just underwent plastic surgery. He pushed me and we prepared for the grand opening.

Although everything was going smooth with the business. Life was present. I would never forget the time I was with a client in the Tallahassee Mall parking lot. The client drove from out of town to visit us. It was challenging giving him the direction to the new store, so I meet him at a common location. Upon his arrival, I received a phone call and we gathered at the store. I didn't know what to expect. From Will voice, I knew it was not going to be anything good. He told me, "I'm just about to come up there." When he arrived, he said someone was in a bad accident. Dee and Montay was there throughout this process. We didn't know who was in the accident or the outcome. We heard it was our brother Trevor, but we were not sure. The client called to tell me he arrived. Will and I headed to the Mall. I went to the back of the truck and began to show the clients our items. He scrolled through our Instagram and began to select designs. Will hit the dashboard. I remained calm and told the client, "We just found out my little brother died." The client responded, "Yeah but I want that one bruh." A voice spoke to me and said work through your hardest times. I heard the last words Trevor echo throughout my head, "You my biggest inspiration bruh... How we were in the streets... How your life was and how you changed it completely around... Can you take me under your wing bruh…?" Those words will stick with me forever. All these thoughts were present as I made sure the client was able to get his grill. I felt numb but focused on the task at hand. I got his address and receipt. I couldn't loss composure. Once I got back into the car, I looked at Will. Will was slumped over in a daze. I pulled out of Tallahassee Mall parking lot, turned left on North Monroe Street and headed South. Distressed and devastated, I said, "Everybody see the success, but they don't know how hard it gets…"

I just received a text message from my brother, Jamaul Vickers. He said, "I miss Trevor man." This is deeper than a book or literature. I called him to let him know I was literally writing about Trevor. Out of the 4000+ minutes in this book, he texted me during the paragraph about Trevor's death. I don't believe in coincidences. Jamaul and I do not communicate daily. This was my first time talking to him about Trevor since he has been out of prison. He actually spoke to Trevor the day he passed. I was not aware of the conversation. Trevor spirit still lives through many of his family, friends, and loved ones. This was confirmation.

A week later, we moved the remaining furniture in the store an hour before his funeral. I remember speeding on the backroad in the U-Haul truck. I passed his funeral, went home to change clothes then came back to walk him out of the church. In life, you just have to keep your head up and do what you have to do #LongLiveTrevorChambers. As a big brother and leader, my job is never complete. I am always focused on becoming the best version of myself to motivate others around me. I lost so many loved one on this journey. I don't want to lose anyone else. I named this chapter

Collective Triumph because this was a victory for our community. After all the setbacks, fights, shootouts, convictions, loses, deaths, odds stacked against us, we were able to do something positive and inspire everyone to chase their dreams.

On March 16, 2016, I posted a status on Facebook stating, "I've been operating for 11 months and I'm proud to say I'm 21 and a successful black business owner. I want to thank all my supporters, family, and friends for helping me. I want to inspire everyone to chase their dreams regardless of how hard times get and keep GOD first. Always have faith and be disciplined enough to receive your blessings. Be patient and wait to receive your blessing because everything comes with a price. Sometimes it's your freedom or even your life. Stay humble every step of the way and if you can help others don't hesitate. I will inspire and show others how to get their businesses started. I will show them how to keep faith and how to keep GOD 1st. This is just the beginning."

One of my life missions is to help everyone reach their full potential. I believe leading by example is an effective form of leadership. Since the launch of Delevoe's Lobby, LLC storefront in 2016, I've seen a massive amount of successful young black owned businesses open and flourish in our community. The rate of entrepreneurs has increased. Support within college, local, and other communities has increased. Our plaza is completely full of thriving businesses. Entrepreneurship is great for the economy. Entrepreneurs create jobs. Entrepreneurs give back to the community via events, inspirations, workshops, and more. It's a struggle being an entrepreneur. However, it's a struggle being a single parent. It's a struggle growing up in public housing. It's a struggle keeping a job. It's a struggle becoming a man without a man present. It's a struggle surviving after inspirational trauma. It's a struggle battling mental health issues. It's a struggle not to become a statistic. It's a struggle to keep bills play without a steady income. It's a struggle getting along when everybody is stressing. It's a struggle being a leader when you're under attack. It's a struggle raising a man when you're a woman. It's a struggle putting money on the phone and canteen when your rent is due. It's a struggle finding resources when everyone needs the same resource. Embrace your struggles to unlock your full potential. Your struggles are your very own unique treasure. Pure as gold, shiny as silver, hard as a diamond, precious as gemstone and exclusively yours. We are a collection of rare diamonds forming under life intense pressures and heat.

JOURNEY QUOTES

"If you can't fly, then run, if you can't walk run, then walk, if you can't walk, then crawl, but by all means keep moving forward." – *Martin Luther King, Jr.*

"The key to realizing a dream is to focus not on success but significance, and then even the small steps and little victories along your path will take on greater meaning."– *Oprah Winfrey*

"We are what we repeatedly do. Excellence, then, is not an act but a habit."– *Aristotle*

"We are at our very best, and we are happiest when we are fully engaged in work, we enjoy on the journey toward the goal we've established for ourselves. It gives meaning to our time off and comfort to our sleep. It makes everything else in life so wonderful, so worthwhile." - *Earl Nightingale*

"Sometimes we make the process more complicated than we need to. We will never make a journey of a thousand miles by fretting about how long it will take or how hard it will be. We make the journey by taking each day step by step and then repeating it again and again until we reach our destination." *- Joseph B. Wirthlin*

"I grew up with an older brother, and the bond between siblings is unlike anything else, and it can be a real journey to accept what that bond is once you both mature into it. Because it's not always what you want. It's not always what you expect. It's not always what you imagined or hoped. But it's one of the most important things in the world." *- Ben Schnetzer*

"Humans have a light side and a dark side, and it's up to us to choose which way we're going to live our lives. Even if you start out on the dark side, it doesn't mean you have to continue your journey that way. You always have time to turn it around." *- Taraji P. Henson*

"Success is about dedication. You may not be where you want to be or do what you want to do when you're on the journey. But you've got to be willing to have vision and foresight that leads you to an incredible end." *– Usher*

"Everything is an open book. I don't speak on other people's hardship, but if it happened in my life or something that has been an experience on my particular journey, I'm going to talk about it. That's what my fan base appreciates the most. I'm universal. You can relate to the things I say or that I go through."

- Kevin Hart

5

REHABILITATION

THE HONORABLE LOUIS FARRAKHAN boldly declared, "And I hope that five years and ten years from now, I'll be a better man, a more mature man, a wiser man, a more humble man, and a more spirited man to serve the good of my people and the good of humanity." I believe to become a better man; one must want to be a better man. I believe to become a more mature man; one must accept responsibility as a man. I believe to be a wiser man; one must become a student of life. I believe to be a humbler man; one must face setbacks, failures, and adversities to recognize room for growth. I believe to be a more spirited man; one must nourish and heal from any struggles, obstacles, or mishaps. I would love to stand on the shoulders on the Honorable Louis Farrakhan to boldly declare and speak life. I have love, faith, hope, and believe that this generation and generations to come will become better humans, will become mature in GOD's love, will become wiser, will become more humble, will personally grow and self-develop a righteous spirit to serve each other without looking for anything in return, and for the overall good of humanity. I declare and speak life over our community. I declare and speak life throughout households. I declare and speak peace throughout the nations. I declare and speak protection over my brothers and sisters. I declare and speak knowledge, wisdom, and understanding into our minds. I declare and speak generational wealth, favor, abundance, freedom, and prosperity into our hearts. I declare and speak purity, cleanliness, virtues, forgiveness, love, faith, and hope into our souls.

In this chapter, I will write letters to relatable struggles, naturally deceased family members and loved ones, incarcerated family members, and select leaders who has helped empower and strengthen me during character building moments. This chapter is very personal. My therapist recommended I write a letter to my abusers. Initially, I declined. Later, I recognized a problem. I was running subconsciously. So, I made a decision. I'm going to allow myself to shine light on the mishaps and I going to acknowledge personal growth and self-development in the process. My mission is to lead by example. I will embrace my vulnerability. Remember, you are not alone. There's nothing new under the sun. Many of us suffer in silence. The goal is to make it count. The goal is to turn negatives into positives. The goal is to overcome. Your situation did not start with you. Listen, you experience situations, but you are not your situation. You are not your situation. You are not a victim. You are more than enough. We are still here. We are still impactful. We still are alive. We still have strength. We still have power and abilities. We still have purpose. We still have GOD. We have the most powerful abundant source known to man. Someone is still suffering. We must show other brothers and sisters' tactics, safe remedies, and formulas to create a positive fulfilling life. There are ways to get your emotions out. There are ways to fight the voices in your head. There are ways to overcome struggles. May the letters on the next pages serve as example for your letters.

I challenge everyone reading or listening to write letters. You can use the topics examples or uniquely craft it to fit your life. Writing letters will help you regain mental control, connect with others, identify learned behaviors, release bottled emotions, experience deep gratitude, and many lives changing phenomenon. I actually wrote 75% of my letters before typing this introduction. Doing so, helped me vividly express benefits in integrity. Remember, you are the master of your abilities. Remember, you are the captain of your fate. Remember, life happened for you not to you. Embrace your struggles to unlock your full potential. We are not perfect, but our imperfection makes us unique. Our imperfections connect us with other humans.

I decided to embrace the process and tackle everything at once. I didn't know the process would take me on an emotional roller-coaster. I cried, burst out in joy, relapsed into a minor depression, patted myself on the back, laid in bed in the fetal position, yelled out loud, laugh, and cried tears while snot running down my nose. I embraced the pain. I was all over the place. However, I felt connected with something inside of myself. I felt my soul connecting with parts that were locked away. I felt connected by my inner spirit and found inner strength. Here's a GEM: *True desire from the heart is a sign of GOD.* It was in my heart to write these letters. GOD knew I had some healing and growing to do. If you never deal with a situation, it follows you throughout your life. I do have a desire for these struggles to follow me. I'm leading and leaving the struggles. I'm leaving the pain. I'm leaving guilt. I'm embracing them in a positive way. I'm leaving the negative behind. You have to learn when to let go of things that's not adding value to your life. These letters below is a reflection of my dedication to personal growth and self-develop into the best version of myself. They are raw, unedited and unpolished. This is directly out of the mind of 24-year-old Patrice L. Delevoe Jr., Jay D, and P.J thoughts. Those are my top three personalities, spirits, and identities.

Dear Doubts, Fears and Uncertainties,

I have dreams to live. I have goals to accomplish. I have a life to fulfill. I have examples to set. I do not have time to allow your negative thought to influence me to be average. I was not sent here to be average. I was sent here to lead. I was sent here to break generational curses. If I was average, I would not have made it to my mothers' egg. The odds have been stacked against me since birth. Why would I doubt myself now? Why should fears enter now? How can I be uncertain now?

I'll tell you why… Because you are all storytellers. You like to find someone who is phenomenal and create senses of insecurity. You are amongst the loudest voices in most individuals head. The thought telling them us, we can't achieve. The thought telling us to call others to see if they will boost us up to try something new. The thought motivating us to procrastinate longer. The thought that's telling us were not good enough. The thought that's telling us we are not ready to go to the next level. All those thoughts are centered around mediocre.

Over generations, you have increased. But here's a GEM: *"For where your treasure is, there your heart will be also"*. This scripture was located in the Holy Bible in Matthew chapter 6 verse 21. On my journey towards my personal legend, I got closer the farther I got away from each one of you. I was fearless with clear intentions. I was bold without apology.

I was in pursuit without question. I was hungry. I had a GPS on my treasure. I knew exactly where my treasure was located. I was certain. I knew it because it was closest to my heart. I stand in integrity when I make this statement. You try to enter my mind, but you are not a part of my heart.

At times, I became confused because I didn't know the distinction between the two. I'm going to show you what I learned. I learned the power of habits. I consciously removed you for my thoughts. Anytime you tried to enter, I rejected you like a toll-free number. I kept this up for over 30 days. It was challenging but I created this positive habit. I didn't want you to be a part of my life anymore. Wow, I love the power of positive thinking. Here's the truth, even with positive habits you still find a way to slitter in. You're a snake.

Much love and recognition to Mel Robbins, she crushed you with the 5 second rule. She literally broke every particle in your nonexistent body. Your biggest weakness is quick and precise decision making. Neither of you like decision makers. Neither of you like individuals who are confident with their decision making. Neither of you like true leaders. You don't like us. You pray on us as amateurs or rookies until we become professionals and masters. We learn how to beat you. We learn how to use you for motivation. We learn how to recognize and acknowledge your existence. We know when you're present. So, we shut you out before you enter. We are very deliberate and intentional.

Learning to listen to my inner spirit and GOD granted me the ability to ignore each one of you. My faith, hope, and love did not leave room for you. My mental capacity was filled with positive vibrations. I learned to meditate to quiet the negative thoughts. I recognized the mind, body, and soul alignment was necessary to enhance my focus. Doubt is out of alignment. Fear is out of alignment. Uncertain is out of alignment. Therefore, each of you must leave. I am a King. A King is not an effective leader if he's drowning in doubts, fears, and uncertainties.

Courageously,
A FEARLESS BRAVE LION

Dear Peer Pressure,

Wow, I really allowed you to take me on some journeys. I wouldn't be the person I am today if I didn't allow you to win sometimes. I've gained much knowledge, wisdom, and understanding from each experience. I know how you work now, so good luck trying to take me out. I always heard pressure does two things, bust pipes or form diamonds. The peer pressure I experienced formed diamonds. I have many nieces, nephews, children, and more generations growing up who will experience you. My advice to them will be to follow their instincts, reflect on lectures, and trust their intuition.

To be completely honest, nine times out of ten I knew when I was doing something wrong. For example, my first time getting arrested. We were coming down the road heading to fun station. We turned into fun station only to find some guys from another city mugging us, throwing up signs, and other indications of aggression. My intuition told me, "We should just go to the other party." However, peer pressure leads us to park and head to the fun station. I will not disclose all the details of this event. I don't know if I remember it completely.

I do know peer pressure was involved. I went against my own judgement to make sure a situation was handled the "right" way. This affected future opportunities. For example, I was not able to join the AirForce due to the charge. It was a juvenile charge, but it still affected opportunities.

The situation had escalated so quickly there was nothing we could have possibly done other than avoid the event altogether. This lesson taught me things about you that I never learned in school.

Do you remember when I was heading to the club with a group of my friends? I was not even old enough to get into the club. I was not drinking yet. I did not smoke. However, the car was filled with smoke and we had open containers. As a teenager, I was under the impression that everything was good. My mother would tell me not to smoke in the car. Sometimes, I had it under control. Sometimes, I would not say anything because I didn't want to "kill the vibe". This experience helped me understand why I don't allow you to win anymore.

We got pulled before turning into Bajas parking lot on Pensacola Street in Tallahassee. The peers who were in the car with me began to panic. The officer came to the window and I was the driver, so I became responsible for everything. We stepped out of the car and they began to search the car. During the search, an open bottle was found, a marijuana blunt, and other objects. Nobody knew who owned any of these items. I was the driver, so everything was my responsibility. The officers explained how I'm responsible for the items that's in my car. The items were in plain sight. They didn't even try to hide it.

I was a minor. The officer called my mother and explained the situation to her. She was furious and disappointed altogether. This was a birthday night, but it ended early. The vibe was killed. I explained to the officers they did not have permission to search the car because it was not my car. The situation worked out in our favor. We were released after sitting in the parking lot of the club, no charges were filed, and the officers didn't have to a long file. I realized an ugly reality. You are not my friend peer pressure. I cannot allow you to control my future or risk my future. This is only a couple examples, but I have learned many lessons.

Sincerely,
A YOUNG ADOLESCENT

Dear Addictions,

You seem to change so much while staying constant. You appear in different forms such as products, situations, and quantities but remain constant in trying to fill my void. I have identified your toxicity but still fall victim to your traps. Over the years, my strength has increased. I have gained a sense of self-reliance. Surviving situations enhanced my mindset and amplified my wisdom. I asked, "GOD grant me the serenity to accept the things I cannot change, the courage to change the things I can, and the wisdom to know the difference." I am a product of my decisions not my circumstances. I am a brave, courageous leader. I am a positive example. I have the power and courage to change my realities. I was sent to break generational curses. Coach Stormy helped recognize, I am the ambassador of my bloodline. I repeated these affirmations daily.

I have changed my reality. I saw the negative effects of you Addiction. I saw our reality. Temporary fix for an ongoing problem. I learn how to dig up the root. It's exhausting battling a problem without acknowledging it. The first step is acknowledging you instead of denying you. I've treated you like you didn't exist. Then I began to form a plan of action against you. It was hard letting you go at first. I made a vision board of my goals. Addictions were not on there, so I stayed focused on the vision. You are a distraction. It was so easy to come back to you. You actually made me relapse a few times. I used to feel horrible when relapsing, but I learned it was a part of the process. For example, I've beaten my drug addiction. You aimed to cloud my vision. There was a time when I didn't understand my next steps because I was chemically altered.

I was addicted to relationships. I thought I needed someone else to love me to feel complete. I was addicted to sex. I liked the pleasure without the commitment. I was addicted to money. I thought it could solve all my problems. I was addicted to drinking. I wanted to drink all my pain away. I was addicted to fame. I wanted everyone to know me. You echoed throughout my life. You made it difficult for me to get along with anyone. A problem does not seem like a problem until you notice it affects you and others. I never had bad intentions. I never wanted to hurt anyone, but you have been the cause of others pain.

I'm healing now Addiction. GOD and I have been working to defeat you. He has equipped me with my tools, resources, and strategies. As I continue to embrace the process, I now look forward to keeping you in the past. I'm leaving you behind. There's no room in my life for you. You're nothing but a bad habit. It takes 21 days to break a habit. I've learned how to build and destroy habits. If I remove a bad habit, I have to add a great habit to create balance. The more positive habits I form, the less I see you.

Without you, I'm doing things I never imagined. I'm networking with like-minded individuals. I'm focused on my goals completely. I'm not worried about you. I opened my first store. I have people in my life who I love, and they love me back. I can't believe I allowed myself to be attached to you. This is my detachment. I never want to see or hear from you again. Just for the record, I'm going to let the world know how horrible you are.

Goodbye Addiction,
A CHANGED MAN

Dear Anxiety and Stress,

I'm so tired of you. I'm tired of you trying to take my family, friends, and loved ones away from me. I'm tired of you thinking you have the ability to dictate my future. I'm tired of you thinking you have enough power to control me. I'm tired of allowing you to block my blessings. I've observed you destroy so many homes, marriages, friends, and other beautiful coalitions. I know your weakness. She is the sister of wisdom. She is the cousin of mercy. She has the ability to move mountains. Her name is faith.

Once I learned to have faith, my anxiety and stress levels decreased. I've been leading by example to eliminate you from everyone's mind, heart, and spirit. Positive energy beats you every time. I learned e-motion means energy in motion. This is significant because now I'm up one on you. If I begin to stress or gain anxiety, I just work out or celebrate like I won a few million dollars. This releases positive signals to my brain. Thank you for the tips Tony Robbins. He came out to do a speech and dominated the stage. He helped equip us with tools against you.

This has led me to do more research, observe, and follow individuals who is beating this curse I will not allow you to turn my hairs gray or make me age early. I have a long life to live. I will not allow you to terminate it early. Somewhere along the line, you have been there to push me forward. However, this form of motivation is not healthy. I have found other ways to fuel my drive. I watched my loved ones and friends stress over things they could not control. I want everyone to reach their full potential. Y'all are not the answer to anyone's problems.

Now, I have your attention. I want to make you an offer. You must understand how to come in moderation. Slight anxiety for celebrations, maybe a little stress to push me forward. I just don't need you to overwhelm me. You don't own me. I own me. If you can't come in moderation, I have no choice but to leave you. My most important goals are centered around health, wealth, family, freedom, and love. I'm trying to find a way to squeeze you in.

Over the past few years, I've been working towards my goals. I have been beating many odds. I have been taking risks and pursuing my dreams without noticeable doubt. You have been working towards making me feel like I'm not maximizing. However, my result is exceptional. Sometimes, I lose sight of my own life. I'm taking my power back. I will not allow you to drain me. I will not allow you to overpower me. I am in control. I will only allow you to enter in a positive light. So, I take my offer back.

Here's the deal: This is my life. I am the master of my abilities. I am the captain of my faith. I will make positive decision without the influence of stress. I will stay on track without focusing on anxiety. I will take time daily to meditate so my energy will align with my mind, body, and spirit. Doing so, I will spread positive and uplifting energy to my family, friends, and loved one. If you find your way back into my life, you will be controlled by my consciousness. I appreciate all the time we have shared. You are not required to respond to this message. This is for my own personal clarity. Oh yeah, stay away from my family, friends, and loved one. This message is not only for this generation. This goes down to my grandchildren and many generations to come. Stay away!

Thanks in advance,
ANXIETY & STRESS-FREE ADVOCATE

Dear Bullies,

I should beat you up now that I have more skills. I'm still trained to go upside your head. I'm laughing out loud but to be honest I appreciate each and every one of you. You really helped me gain tough skin. Once I entered the real world, I was prepared for anything. I hope you find fulfilment and meaning in your life. I was really battling some serious things while dealing with your belittlement. I forgive you for you did not know. I give you the benefit of the doubt. If you have any kids, I suggest you raise them to be humane. I thought something was wrong with me, but I was not the one with issues. I had to learn more about myself. I had to learn more about my "girl" first name. "To whom much is given, much is required." My name is passed down from great leaders. Once I learned this, I got over the weak jokes. I had to learn more about my melanin. Being black is not bad. It's actually powerful. Did you know Melanin has special powers? Look it up if you don't believe me.

I know I may look slightly different. Some of my family is from Bahamas and Africa. I was put into speech classes when I was younger. The instructors identified a speech impediment. I'm actually appreciated for my speaking now. Here's the moral of the story, you bullies were only able to get under my skin because I did not understand who I was. Once I self-actualized, a King appeared instead of a child struggling with his identity. I'm thankful for each and every one of you. You forced me to dig deeper to learn how to appreciate features I could not change.

Listening to Lil Boosie, Crime Mob, Webbie, and many other artists helped me gain the mindset to ignore haters. I learned how to gain the courage to fight back instead of allowing you all make me feel less. My brothers and the neighborhood made sure I was trained on joking, protecting myself, and any other tactics for y'all. People would always say, "Stick and stones may break my bones, but words can never hurt me." Words actually did hurt at first especially when coming from people you thought were pretty cool. Y'all good though. I learned how to be fearless, courageous, and brave.

I really walked around mad at the world. I was ready to fight anybody as a protective mechanism. My hand or foot was the only thing able to conceal your mouth. I remember I used to get picked on for having old tennis shoes on during dress out day. I decided to wear brown or black shoes like regular days. I didn't have Jordan's but I do remember the jokes. I wanted to fit in with y'all so bad. My value system was wrapped around being popular. Initially, I was denied. There are so many incidents but thank you. I'm proud of the person I've become. I'm actually stronger, wiser, and very successful.

I wish each and every one of you the best of luck in life. I genuinely want to see you succeed and reach your full potential. I'm going to give you the benefit of the doubt.

As stated earlier, make sure you raise your kids with great values. I could have been psycho and came to school with one of my brothers' guns to shoot you. That's not GOD love. I'm happy I was raised in a loving environment. You should be happy too. I was listening to a motivational video and the speaker said, "GOD removed you from that circle to change your life." I was young but I remember the circle didn't have everyone's best interest at heart. I forgive everyone who has played a role in my experience of being bullied.

Honestly,
NEIGHBORHOOD PROJECT BABY

Dear Health Issues,

I've watch you generationally destroy families. I've seen you come in so many forms such as cancer, AIDS, diabetes, and so forth. However, Dr. Sebi provided education and healing for more than 40 years. I began to research cures and effective methods to eliminate you. You reign of generational defeat and affliction has come to an end. I've lost weight and became so much healthier myself. I'm glad I researched. I grew up loving pig meat such as bacon, pork chops, pork neckbones, and other southern favorites. I did not know the pig did not sweat. This seems like a small thing until I learned a pig will eat anything. When we sweat, our toxins leave our body. The pig does not sweat so toxins spread throughout its flesh. When a pig is slaughtered pus leaks from its flesh. I was disgusted by this. You enter our bodies through our food. Changing my lifestyle to defeat health issues was not the easiest process. My ways for overcoming had to be bigger than the excuses. As I thought about it, the food taste good. However, it had a negative effect on my body.

My grandfather Raymond Wilcoxson died from prostate cancer. I never got to meet him. I will not allow you to take me out before I meet my grandkids. I will continue defeating you with positive food choices and work out habits. I work out now. I started by doing short runs. I can jog and run up to 4 miles now. This is just the beginning. I will run marathons to inspire others. The Honorable Nipsey Hussle explained the difference between a race and a marathon. In my understanding, a marathon continues without stopping. Changing habits for a short period of time is similar to running a race. I decided to beat you by changing and building long term positive habits. This is my way to allow the marathon to continue #TMC I will continue to push myself beyond my limits.

I've been on numerous water and fruit fast. My maximum amount of day was three so far. The first day I felt drained. I think my body was detoxing during this phase. I was always taught energy came from food. I was surprised when I had a burst of energy the second day. I'm still developing my mental, physical, and spiritual muscles. I've learned the concept of mind over matter. I will conquer anything I put my mind too. My goal is to start doing seven days of fasting to keep my mind, body, and soul aligned.

My Grandmother Dr. Delevoe has an alkaline diet. She studies Dr. Sebi and only eats the foods approved on his list. Did you know our body has the ability to heal itself? Dr. Sebi cured so many diseases such as AIDS, cancer, herpes, and so forth. I'm sure you know this Health Issues. He was a major threat to you. My Grandmother leads by example. Her testimony is so powerful because she defeated you. Doctors tried to prescribe her medication numerous times, but she turned to natural remedies. She inspires me to continue changing my eating habits. I have been changing slowly but surely. I removed pork from my diet. I rarely eat red meat.

My goal is to have an alkaline lifestyle. It's a challenge but this goal will grant me the ability to grow and develop into a healthy seasoned man.

I will grow old with a healthy mind, body. and soul. I will be able to travel, speak, think, and play with my great grandchildren. I must embrace my struggle to remove negative foods. I must unlock my full potential by intaking positivity charged foods. I will defeat you. I will not allow my family to pick up the same habits I received from other generations. Health is wealth.

Sincerely,
ASPIRING HOLISTIC HEALTH COACH

Dear Financial Challenges,

Growing up in Havana's neighborhood projects, I thought you were an incurable disease. I thought you were going to be an everlasting part of my life. I thought we were going to be married until death do us apart. It seemed like I would get money, spend it, and find you back into my life. I could never escape you. I would receive a paycheck, pay out, or investment only to see you hiding behind the obligations. You are the father of struggle. I vowed to remove you out of my life. I got tired of the negative thoughts associated with your presence. I saw others who did not suffer from you. I knew I had the potential to remove you. My first thought was going to school so I can find a job pay at least 6 figures. 6 figures would remove parts of my struggle.

Once I flunked out of college and lost my scholarships, you emerged without hesitation.

I watched a YouTube Video and Warren Buffet said, *"The more you learn, the more you earn."* I began to emerge myself in Millionaires Mindset Academy. He was telling the truth. You are only a negative habit. You are not powerful. You are not permanent. You are a limiting belief. I came to many realizations about you. Imagine one of your biggest enemies turning out to be a fraud. Well look in the mirror Financial Challenges. You are the image in the mirror.

You were only an illusion. The more I forgot you exist the less you appeared. I listened to Rich Dad, Poor Dad and

Think and Grow Rich. They completely put you to rest. I became aware of the opportunities that surround me. There's not a lack of opportunity. I have family, friends, loved ones, and business partners who want to see me in a winning position. I've learned how to pay attention; be the energy I want to receive and trust the process. The cure to beating you was aligning myself with my dreams, visions, and goals. I had to take action against you. It was not an easy process because I experienced you appearing into my life more than I want to admit.

Once I acknowledged you, I saw ways to remove you. I stopped my negative habits such as overspending at the club, eating expensive meals daily, and going over budgets without caring. A wise man once said, "It's not about how much money you make but how much you keep." The way I was spending it was hard to keep much of my earning after expenses. I began to pay closer attention. The easy way to beat you is to take 10%-15% out of all income as soon as it arrives. Allow the income to build or stack as we call it in the neighborhood. This money is now considered capital. I know you hate capital Financial Struggles. Capital is your enemy. Capital has the ability to generate systems. The systems can wipe you out for generations to come. I learned this from many financial gurus. You're not as strong as I thought you were. I learned how to manage money the wrong way. I give gratitude and appreciate Millionaires Mindset Academy, Audible, YouTube, Google Search engine and other information sources for allowing me to bury you. Your time has come to an end. I'm on a mission to grant everyone access to blueprints, wealth formulas, coaching, and so forth. P.S. – Excellent credit is a MAJOR key too. You thought I forgot to mention excellent credit but nope it's right here. May you rest in peace. FOREVER!

Boldly,

PATRICE L. DELEVOE JR.

MMA, MILLIONAIRE MENTOR

Dear Depression,

You are so sneaky. You will enter in the mist of the night and creep in like a cheater. You have always aimed to kill, steal, and destroy happiness. You are like a python measuring it prey then viciously suffocating it. I used to keep myself busy to avoid meeting with you. I would endlessly work, fall asleep, and wake up grinding again. This was my coping mechanism. Death triggered you easily. The first time I meet you was when my sister passed in the fifth grade. I dealt with everything else without entering major depression. Death hit me a little different though. I remember being very quiet externally but internally voices crowed my brain. This was out of the ordinary because I engaged with others. My first major taste of you took me on a ride.

I would always tell myself I could have done something different. I felt like I could have changed the situation. Now, I've learned how to embrace my grieving process. It's not easy but it's necessary. I have to fight through it like everything else. It's so easy to walk around like nothing bothers you. It's easy to walk around with a smile on your face but breaking down inside. The hardest part is attacking the issue. It forces you to deal with concealed emotions. When I deal with you, I apply this GEM: *Don't stress over things beyond your control.* You will have an individual focused on things beyond their control.

I made a commitment to myself. I am done allowing resentment and negative emotions to be a part of life. I am taking control and rewriting the narrative. This process has been crucial to the development of my character. My depression was filled with anger. During one period of my depression, I fought back to back to back. I wanted to relieve anger. I was hurt about Chad's death. I didn't have a therapist. I would replay the night over and over. I felt like I was losing myself altogether. A part of me died that night too. You will lead a person to think everyone is against them. You will take over a person's identity. You are like a thief in the night.

When my life fell down, I didn't think I had the strength to get up. I took so many losses on multiple levels. I lost people who were closest to me. I felt disconnected from everyone including myself. I experienced so many setbacks, obstacles, even contemplated suicide but I didn't give up. I learned how to pray and give my problem to GOD. Somehow, I managed to find a GEM: *I can do all things through Christ who strengthens me.* I didn't have a therapist. I learned how to pray. Building a personal relationship with GOD was my tool against you.

Life is not easy. You know that Depression. That's why you prey on those who have little to no faith. You take advantage of nonbelievers. The weak, weary, and confused are your targets. I'm going to warn everyone about you. I had to take a few breaks writing you. You aimed to gain space in my mental capacity while writing this, but I have too much faith. I'm covered in the blood. I am anointed. I am in my deliverance and salvation. There's no room for you in my life. I have defeated you on multiple occasions. I am peacefully detaching from you. I am a survivor and not a victim. You pushed me to what I would have considered my limited, but you couldn't make me jumped of the edge. So, you tripped me and caused me to fall off the edge. I forgive you because I grew wings on the way down. I must annihilate you now. I am done wiping late night tears. I am done smoking and drinking myself to sleep. I am done getting in relationships as a crutch. I was never in this fight alone. I think you forgot. In the midst of your cloud of confusion, I called out like never before. HE APPEARED. Thank you for testing me. I passed.

Kind regards,
AN OLD FRIEND

Dear Suicide,

You will not win. I don't know why you tried to come into my life. I have a purpose, calling, and many potentials. I don't know why you aim to manipulate us. Kings and Queens will reach our full potential. We've been sent to destroy you. We will not fall victim to your deceit. We've seen you face to face. We've beat you time after time. You are not as strong as you think. I've found your weaknesses to be self-worth and self-love. How could you win if someone understands their value and love themselves?

There's no excuse for allowing you to win. In my dark moments, I thought you were the solution to peace. I wanted you to enter my life because I didn't want to feel pain anymore. After pulling myself from those places, I found the light. I learned how to be light. I will not allow you to take my brothers and sisters away. I remember sitting on the floor with a knife in my hand. I remember searching in the bathroom for a bottle of pills. I remember thinking about driving off the road into a tree. I remember each time I was struggling with life battles. When I learned how to give my problems to GOD, I felt a shift in my life. I learned how to identify the root of problems.

I did not connect to my first therapist in college. I tried my best to open up. However, another part of my brain would take over. I would go into a protective mode and only speak on the surface. The therapist was there to help me, but I did not trust my therapist. I did not want to be on any medicine. I did not want my therapist to know I was thinking about you. So, I went home and researched. I thought about you from time to time. I even attempted a couple times. I had to gain emotional intelligence and fast. I came from a background of silence sufferers. In the neighborhood, we are too tough to have any problems. I would smile or a joke through any pain. This would provide a temporary happiness until I was by myself.

To be completely honest, I think I was afraid to be in the presence of myself. I didn't know what to expect. In the depths of my depression, I would allow voices to come from every direction. I would allow one negative thought to turn into hundreds. Sometimes, I was even afraid of the dark. I always felt like something would attack me in the dark. I always wanted to keep a little light to see. Reflecting back, I think this was a result of being touched during my sleep. I'm unsure but it could be a result.

One day I was listening to a YouTube video, this video really impacted my mindset positively. I heard Tony Robbins drop a GEM: *"Life happened for you not to you."* This was very powerful. Often, individuals may look at situations negatively. They feel like situations happen to them. They feel like situations happen to stop them. This is true with a negative mindset. However, a positive mindset views life differently. We feel like situations happen for us to grow from them. We feel like situations happen for us to propel us forward. So, this is why I cannot and will not allow you to win. Your presence has only created a demand for a self-examination. The self-examination will be presented in the next chapter. My life is worth living. My life is valuable. My life is making positive impacts. My life is saving other lives. My life is bringing hope into communities. My life is phenomenal. I'm going to be honest. Kings and Queens don't like you. We only act like we like you when we are going through tough times. Now that we got that out the way, stay away for all of us.

Royally,

KING PATRICE L. DELEVOE JR.

Dear Abusers,

I forgive you…
GOD bless each and every one of you.

Break

I started a letter then deleted it. I'm going to resume instead keeping it short. My entire life was affected by your actions. I viewed things differently from my peers. I struggled with spirits, thoughts, and learned behaviors. I struggled with establishing a relationship with GOD. I always asked him how he could let me go through things like that if he truly loves me. I did not understand what was "wrong" with me. The abuse made it difficult for me to relate to others. The abuse lowered my self-respect and self-worth. I walked around for years thinking I was "okay" but I was not. My relationships would fall apart because a part of me would not trust. I was loving from a place of hurt. I was always aiming to fill voids, gaps, and other dysfunctions. I was not going to address this issue. Dr. Baity gently insisted. She has really inspired me in more ways than I can articulate. We bump heads often, but she really helped me battle you strategically.

Break

This was the last letter to complete. I didn't know what to say. There's not much to say. There's more to do. My actions will include sharing stories to help others, protecting youth, bringing awareness to this issue. I'm not the only say to you. I pray GOD forgives you for you did not know. I pray GOD has mercy on each of your souls. I genuinely forgive you. I didn't even voice your name. I'm still not going to mention your name. Some of you have families and hopeful your life is one track now. One of you died a long time ago. When I found out you died, I recognized the power of GOD. I started to forgive some of you then. Psalm 105:15 in the Holy Bible gives a GEM: "*Do not touch my anointed ones; do my prophets no harm.*" You touched me and caused me harm. I fought so hard to find myself. I was four years old for one of you. I think it came from your learn behaviors. I recognized a pattern of juvenile program, jail, and prison like settings. I'm not giving you all an excuse, but I recognize this pattern in our community. I'm just brave enough and vulnerable enough to say it. I went through it to help bring others through it. It was challenge and tough, but I made it through the storm. I connect and help so many people now. I'm gratitude for this added strength and I pray you get the help you need so you can help others …

Break

I accepted this challenge and put it all behind me now. Glory to GOD

Genuinely,
A MAN OF GOD

Dear Sandrita Youmas,

I was going through some rough times throughout child-hood. Everyone else was moving so fast, focused on life and preoccupied I felt alone sometimes. I was pretty quiet during these times unless I was involving myself into someone else's business. Although, I never fully expressed my social anxiety problems to you. I felt like you knew. I remember when I got into one of my very first serious neighborhood fights. I had to fade Ty. They would not allow me to walk away. I had my cousin Quaybo telling me what to do in one ear and you telling me to stop in the other. I didn't listen because I felt like I had a point to prove. I knew you were disappointed in me because you slam the door and went into the house. Moments later, we were fighting, and he punched me in my nose. I don't remember every detail, but I do remember blacking out. I looked up and his eye was black. The fight ended and I ran to my house.

I told my mom I got into a fight. It was pretty common for kids to disagree and fight. At least, I didn't get beat up or allow anyone to bully me. I didn't tell my mom I was peer pressured into the fight. She always raised me to be a leader. Reflecting back, I probably should've listened to you. Ty and I never became friends again from that day. He got picked at every day for having a black eye. I was young and didn't want to be looked at as soft. I just wanted to earn my respect like everybody else. If I didn't fight him back, I would've been picked on by someone else. They would've labeled me as soft or a push over. I couldn't accept that sis. I hope you can understand.

I still remember running up and down the road from Riverside to our house together. It was a quick run, but we would always be filled with joy and laughter. The bond we shared was unbreakable. I used to be excited coming home from school to play with you. I would go to Aunt Deborah house looking for you. You're one of the reasons Rod, Twon, Dre and Pat became my brothers. It was so funny because everyone began to joke about me liking you. They thought we had something going on because you would come get in bed with me when you were upset with my brother or wanted to nap. We were just comfortable around each other. I remember the time you came and got me when you went joy riding in you mom's car. We were riding out…. Lol

As we got older, things changed, we were already many years apart. I saw you smoking. I told you I couldn't be your friend anymore. I didn't know any better. I was wrong for judging you. I began to treat you differently. I didn't know you were stressing. Thinking back, I remember one time we were racing to the house. You stopped and held your chest, but I didn't think much of it. I was focused on winning the race. You were always a strong fighter. When they told me, you were at Shands Hospital, I knew you were going to be okay. Sometimes, you would get sick, but you would always bounce back.

My mother called me one early morning before school. She said she had something to tell me. I heard it in her voice. Something was not right. I asked, "Uncle Passed?" She told me, "I will tell you when you get from school." I insisted she tell me. I was not expecting her to tell me that you passed away. I was speechless as pain filled every part of my body. We were coming down to see you. I wish I could have seen you for the last time. I wish I could've said my last goodbyes or at least told you how much your friendship meant to me. You were the sister I never had when I was younger, I felt like you actually understood me. Our friendship was short lived, but you taught me how to value people while they are here. Thank you, I will never forget you.

Missing you,
BIG HEAD P.J.

Dear Uncle Dudley,

It's been a while since we talked Unc. I just want to say thank you for being a phenomenal man. My Auntie Jackie really misses you. She's retired now. She has been enjoying her retirement. I've watched both of you be strong. You are a strong fighter. I remember getting picked up from school on the days you had dialysis. You never complained or wanted pity. You were stern but very fair. When I was younger, I would come watch you clean fish, make adjustments to your boat, or even mow the yard. You already handled things around the house.

Although you have left your natural body, your spirit lives on. Your daughter Ms. Sandy has become another mother to me. She sends messages to boost my spirit with an Inspirational Vitamin. From the first day we meet, she has been a motivational force in my life. Your grandson Madison became my brother. I'm proud of his growth and accomplishments. One day we are going to create something phenomenal to make positive impacts in the world. Deuce has graduated. He still cool as ever. Mr. Marcus is still keeping a smile on Ma Sandy face. I'm grateful I had the opportunity to share moments with you before your departure. May you continue to rest in peace. We love and miss you.

Sincerely,

P. J.

Dear Bruce Lovett,

What's Good Pop… It's been a minute. I would like to thank you for everything you have done for me over the years. You were a great example of a hardworking, warm hearted, leader and father figure. I've heard so many great stories about you since you left. You really did have a heart of gold. You wanted to see everybody happy. I have a better understanding for many of the things you did for me during my childhood. I still remember going to my Grandmother house on Christmas to pick up my gift. I was one of the only kids in the neighborhood with a scooter. I was able to scroll with the big boys. It was so fast and fun. I asked for one, but I knew they were expensive. I didn't actually expect to get one.

I appreciate you for taking me on the road with you to show me how to unload a flatbed. We would get up early mornings to unhook the hinges and straps. I was able to earn some money for things I wanted. I always wanted to buy something. I used to want fireworks, crab legs, the latest clothes, and posters from the book fair. Reflecting back, I know you were overpaying me. I was so determined to do my best. Henny became one of my favorite drinks to sip. It's ironic because I always told you to stop drinking.

I appreciate the time you took me to school in your new Escalade and Corvette. It inspired me to dream bigger and intensified my hunger. I'm grateful for the times I was able to wash them and drive them down the road too. Small things like that build something in a kid. I did not want to settle. I knew I could earn anything I would like to apologize for missing your funeral. I was just coming out of a long depression. I wanted to remind you how I remembered you. That's not an excuse but it's the truth. I was young when you passed. I was only 13 years old. Many valuable lessons are instilled.

As for now, I'm running, building, and developing businesses. Your nephew Gabriel Lovett and I are great business partners. We're creating billion dollar businesses. We will purchase estates and yachts. Please watch over us as we continue to grow and develop our companies. Send us signs and guide us in the right directions. You know how them devils come to kill, steal, and destroy. We go to church, steadfast in faith, and pray throughout the process.

Dallas finding his way out here too. He's growing into a great young man. He's hard working and talented too. Big Bro Bruce Jr. doing well. I went to visit him when he stayed in Houston. It was a great experience. We are elevating and creating a legacy for ourselves.

Mr. Ricky kept his word to make sure I was straight until I became an adult. He tried his best to show me the game. He's wise and shared much knowledge with me. He has a great heart. He likes to talk mess when he's under the influence but all in all, he's a great person. He also helped install the floors into Delevoe's Lobby storefront. I'm going to come to your burial site to talk to you in person. Thanks for pouring into me. I pour into others the same way you poured into me.

Much Respect,
P.J. "BLACK"

Dear Grandmother Odessa Wilcoxson,

I miss you Grandma… It has not been the same since you left. I miss coming to your house to drink sweet tea. I miss seeing you play with your plants. I even miss hearing you yell at us. There are so many things I miss about you. I remember when you showed me the garden in the back. I enjoyed spending days up there with you. I learned so many things from you. You are part of my inspiration to become a farmer. I'm so grateful for you.

You always motivated me to push towards my goals. You would give me money for having great grades in school. I was very fortunate to have you in my corner. I've been pushing Grandma. It hurt me when you left here. I thought you were going to come back home. I learned to work through my hardest times. I was in the Links Beautillion program when you passed away. I tried my hardest to smile and laugh through the painful experiences. The curriculum helped me grow and develop into a gentleman. I know you would be very proud of me. I've been representing the family and will continue to spread the love you instilled in us.

Anytime I hear the song, "Green Onions" by Booker T & The MG's I have flashbacks of how you got up and danced at your 90th birthday party. You really gave everyone a show. You stepped like you was back in the 60s. I'm still learning how to step like the family. You had the whole family up dancing in our royal purple outfit. I'm so happy we had this celebration of life. We did not expect you to leave us early. You lived a long life. I was expecting you to reach 100. You always told us; you were going to reach 100. I know you are still here in spirit. We had a celebration for Uncle Larry birthday. I can still hear your voice when I walk telling us to close the door.

Everyone is doing well. They're retired or running their own business. Uncle Harry is not home right now. I'm praying for him to come home. We miss you though Grandma. You and Grandfather really started a village. Our family has multiplied many times since the birthday of my aunts and uncles. We value family relationship. I watch my mother have conference calls with my aunts on Sundays. I see the love shared during family events amongst the family. Thank you for being healthy and strong enough to create us. We love you so much. Your grandchildren and great grandchildren are working very hard to continue to build upon everything created for us. We appreciate all of your sacrifices. We appreciate your leadership. We thank you for keeping our family in the church. It's reflected through each and every one of our homes. We practice spreading GOD's love.

I was emotional at first when I began writing this letter. However, I realized you made a significant impact. The impact you made created a loving village. You lived a long life. You did not pass with a painful death. Your spirit is spread throughout our family. Now, you are able to spend time with Grandfather Raymond again. I never saw you remarry or even date another man. I'm know he was waiting on you and missed you dearly. I'm going to work on taking out time to come see you and Granddad more often. I love you so much. I miss you. I miss playing with your arms too. I'm going to keep pushing to make you proud. I know you are here with me in spirit. Thanks for all the joy, knowledge, wisdom, discipline, and love you brought to each and every one of us.

Sincerely Yours,
GRANDSON P.J.

Dear Chadric "Liil Chad" Anderson,

You changed my life forever cousin. I never meet some-body that was down to ride as hard as you. I remember times when I would be able to let some good and you would slap somebody down. I used to think you were playing until the situations began to unfold. It felt so different with you here. Everybody missing you man. Nobody has been the same since that night. It's still a nightmare. I wish I would keep you in the car with me. Every time I see ma, I just hugged her. She's still holding up strong. When we found out you didn't make it, we were at a loss for words. I still remember it like it was yesterday. I was praying you would get up when Big Chad was saying "Get up boy!" Your life has positively impacted me. I've changed my life for the better. Most of us changed our lives for the better.

I'm not completely over your death. I don't think I would ever been completely over your death. But I allow it to push me. I allow it to move me forward. I allow it to empower me. I had a fear of public speaking my whole life. My first time embracing the process of speaking was on your 22nd birthday. It's phenomenal because it was not even on purpose. It was in a church too. The kids thought I was a rapper, preacher, or lawyer. They actually listened and received the words. I told them the importance of using their brains instead of their hands. I told them I didn't like fighting anymore. You know where we came from cousin. You know how we use to do back in the days.

Your little sister and brother are not little anymore. Jari in high school now and Journey is almost in middle school. I remember when she was a baby. They miss you so much. AJ getting old too. Everybody been saying focused for the most part. The boys having kids left and right. We are starting businesses and bossing up. I know you would've been first in line. You would have your own business booming by now. I'm trying to finish this letter but honestly, I'm just at a loss for words man… I will continue to talk about you. You name will live on. You did not live in vain. You left your natural body, but your spirit will live on forever. I just wish I could have protected you more cousin. I just hope you can come back for one day or something. All of us are just left with funny memories.

Grandma and I got close before she came up with you. She would always come to the shop. We would hug and talk. We would have our mini photoshoots. She would leave smiling from ear-to-ear. Those were some of the best moments. I just miss you cousin. I miss pulling up on you after school. I miss watching you and Ma go back and forth. I miss going to games, events, hanging out in general. Thanks for believing in me too. You would always hype me up to go harder. You would record me or take pictures of me to show me so I would get more hyped. I remember someone stole my chain from Dee house and you got it back from him at school. So many memories but I'm out here going hard for the family cousin. We're not going to allow your name to go in vain. I'm going to drop something exotic for you. I'm going to accomplish the things we talked about. I'm going to continue to make you proud. I know you have everybody up there in heaven laughing. One day, I'll be up there to share some laughs. I know you're watching over me and continuing to guide me on this journey.

Sincerely,
P.J., JAY D, AND DELEVOE

Dear DJuante "Tae Tae" Tucker,

We are missing you down here big bru. I remember the first time we meet in Macon gym. I thought I was going to have to fade you. You and the whole Northside came through bouncing, pushing, and knocking everyone out of the way. Then, we began to see each other more in the streets. I never expected to get close to you because you were not from my city. We got closer when I started to see you more at Paradise house. I used to get into so much stuff for no apparent reason. I appreciate you for taking me under your wing. I appreciate you for being a genuine friend. During those times, I had many people trying to get cool with me to use me for popularly, material gain, or my kindness. Thank you for pointing out some of those things. You helped me learn how to slide solo. I never felt like love would come from the streets.

Growing up in Havana, Florida and Fort Lauderdale, Florida, I was raised to value family. My family did not make many friends outside of business relationship. The friends became part of the family. Back in the days, Havana and Northside had major beef. Based on code, we were not even supposed to be associates. I remember the night you called me with the whole Northside in the background because you were told we were going to rob you. You came prepared and ready for war. To be real, I was not going to let anybody rob you. That's why I left. Being young and hot headed, some of my friends didn't understand why I looked out for people outside of my neighborhood. I looked out who looked out for me. I remember when rumors would come out about our friendship. People didn't understand it. Everybody was so caught up in separation, division, and negativity their vision was clouded. They failed to realize you showed me genuine love my brother. You actually tried to keep me out of trouble. The energy was pure, and we didn't need each other for anything. That's rare in the streets.

After visiting your home and meeting your family, I realized we shared common background. We came from loving households, high set standards, and above all GOD-fearing parents. We had a solid enriched foundation but choose to engage into neighborhood activities. Mama Jackie is still being strong, helping the community, and beautiful. She's GOD filled and it shows. She helped me get back into New Mt. Zion AME Church. Shuney still Shuney, we actually speak and uplift each other when we see each other now. Janiah has grown up; she's going to be a phenomenal woman. LaKecia is a whole chef and community activist now. Your kids look and act just like you. Everybody is staying strong but misses you. The last few conversations we had stuck with me. I still remember you coming into the apartment with great energy and a bright smile. You told me, "You got something going right here lil bruh, don't stop." Well, I didn't stop bro. I'm still pushing to become the greatest jeweler in the world, working towards becoming the best version of myself and even advocating to stop the violence now. You helped me learn to stop judging others who are not from my own neighborhood. I was doing what I didn't like to be done to me. You help me understand how to be the energy to light up a room. You helped me understand how to be the energy I want to receive. You helped me see that the size of a man is nothing compared to the heart of a man. I'm grateful to have crossed paths with you. Thanks for believing, protecting, guiding, and supporting me.

Anointed,

LIL BROTHER P.J. & JAY D

Dear Trevor "Rich Homie" Chambers,

I still remember our last conversation. The words echo throughout my head, "You're my biggest inspiration bro, would you take me under your wing?" I never got the opportunity to take you under my wing. I think that's why I'm always coaching, mentoring, and teaching now. I'm trying to take everyone under my wing.

Pause

I was stuck for over a week writing your letter bro. I didn't know what to say so I reflected over our messages, I did take you under my wing long before you asked. I guided you to the capacity of my understanding. Do you remember this conversation on January 22, 2013 at 6:53 PM?

You: "but yeah man them chattohoochee boys i took off on 1 of them niggas an the rest of them nigga clicked up an tryed 2 jump me but when i go back 2 school all them nigggas got 2 see me elijah an me was about 2 slide up there in quincy but them niggas going 2 ahve 2 see me an bruh i was the only 1 bumpen when 2 other niggas was right there an they were from havana bruh"

Me: "brah imma tell you like this mane... I done been there and been thru the same shit you goin thru now. honestly, i know you feel like you need to do this to get back and do that to get back but at the end of the day you know what's real and u dnt gotta prove no fuckin point to nobody. dont let them niggas case you up and have you jammed up because they dont got shit goin for they self i love havana n this my hood but im tryna make it out the hood and that's not way to make it out. let them niggas have that shit and jus do u man... focus on yo school shit and make some outta yaself. I know you dun heard this shit ova and ova but it's true lil brah. I wouldn't tell ya nun wrong"

You: "yeah true bruh yeah u right bruh ima just let that shit go bruh i understand"

Me: "fareal man i went thru that same shit......"

I have always been in your ear and corner. I had you under my wing lil brah… I always question myself and asked where I went wrong. After reading the messages, I hit the bed in disappointment because I still lost you. I heard a voice come to me and say, "I'm still right here brah." So, currently I am at peace. I know you are still here with me. I feel your spirit when I'm speaking, introducing somebody to Millionaires Mindset Academy, or driving on the back road.

I remember our conversation after you asked me to take you under my wing. I told you to stay from around him because it was not going to end good. A voice came to me. I was being a vessel. I didn't know until I found out what happened. I wish I had more resources back then to keep you out of situations. You were a phenomenal person with a heart of gold. I remember you telling me you looked up to me, respect me and the extent you would go to protect me. I can truly say even as the little brother you showed me throughout our friendship. Thanks for checking on me when Chad passed even though you were hurting too. I wish I could have done more…

Apologetically,
BIG BROTHER P.J. & JAY D

Dear Darius Davis,

I miss you big bruh… I remember all the late nights we would slide the city. I went to my first entertainer party with you. It was on Mission Road one night with you and T. Larkins. I was only about 15 years old, but it was a great experience. We would go to each of the events until we had no more options. I appreciate you for always looking out for me. You tried your best to keep people from taking advantage of me. So many late nights I would come there tired or under the influence. Your family accepted me in as theirs. You really became my big brother. You pushed me to grind hard, accomplish goals, and develop toughness. I remember coming to you on multiples occasions with ideas and you would tell me, "Do it then bih!" I catch myself saying that sometimes. You were one of my first supporter in the gold business. I remember you telling me, "We on bih!"

Reflecting back, I think you were one of my guardian angels. We would hang out and you would peep things I didn't see. You kept me on my Ps and Qs. Remember when we went to PC in the Charger? Everyone was posted up at the mall and I did a donut while playing Lil Boosie. I used to think I was a mini Lil Boosie. Your face was funny bih, you didn't know I had them skills. I told you to stop sleeping on me. I just wish you were still out here. You little girl is getting so big. Kiesha starting a family and she's a talented entrepreneur. KJ doing his thing, progressing, and growing into a man. Leelee grown now and attacking life head on. Time has been speeding but I know you're still here in spirit.

I was so proud of you when you got your first car. You dropped the Coupe on your own. You told me you were stacking and making it happen. You were running it up. You had so many plans that were beginning to manifest. At times, I'm still in disbelief. It seems like we were just in Hotel Duval for my going away party. I still have those pictures. I got on Facebook to promote the store and I saw a status from Keisha. I didn't believe it at first. We will meet again brother. I'm going to have to fade you for leaving like that. My hands quicker now bih… I'm going to have some raps ready. We should do a feature or two. Yeah, I'm going to get on that bih. Lol but thanks for everything man. You were a real one. They don't make too many like you anymore. You used to say that but it's crazy how I'm saying it now. When I blow, I'm going to make sure the things we talked about are handled. Thanks for believing in me bruh… I'm going to close this one out. Love you my n*gga

Break

I had to take a break writing your letter and tried to cut it off a little early. I came back to finish it. I just want to say Thank you for being a phenomenal brother. Often, we don't appreciate individuals when they're here. We take them for granted or think we have endless time with them. You reminded me everything can change overnight. It's not every day to meet someone as real as you but I'm fortunate enough to have you as a brother. You gained your wings early, but your spirit will live on forever.

Truly,

LIL BRUH P.J.

Dear Grandfathers,

I wish I could have had the opportunity to meet both of you. I have heard so many positive stories. I know if I still had both of you into my life, I would have received more guidance on being a man. Over the generations, the idea of a man has changed. Traditions are not the same. The media, drugs, and government has created so much influence over the past few decades. Single family rates have risen over 50% in the past three decades.

Grandfather Raymond Wilcoxson Sr., you and Grandmother raised a strong, rare family. We have grown to be well known and respected throughout North Florida and South Georgia. We may argue and bicker from time to time, but we are a strong, wise, and blessed family. We come from great stock. My mother misses you. She still talks about your birthday. She talks about the time you whipped her and Auntie Gwen. The story makes me laugh every time. When I went to Midway Magnet, we would stop to visit you time to time. I eat healthier because I was told prostate cancer run in our family. I'm going to make sure it stops here. I'm going to make sure we eat healthy, exercise regularly, and take care of our bodies. My mother told me you were a strong man. You did not allow the family to see you weak or complaining. It shows in my uncles. They do not like for others to see them sweat. I love you Grandpa. I know your genes keep me loving, stern, and on track. Family was very important to you. It's important to me too. Your culture and customs help me recognize value in agriculture, intimate gatherings, and acceptance. Thank you for a solid foundation.

Grandfather Reverend Samuel Delevoe Sr,. you and Grandmother created a legacy throughout South Florida. The shoes are not easy to fill. Instead of trying to fill them, I'm going to stand on both of your shoulders. I have been able to see the world from a different lens. I tapped into some of my inner greatness. I came from Puerto Rico with my dear friend. I stood beside the lake at Delevoe's Park. I could feel your spirit and positive energy. I felt like I heard a voice say, "Keep going, I'm on the right path." I felt connected. We're having your 40th Reverend Samuel Delevoe Day on November 11, 2019. Grandmother told me Bob Graham gave a proclamation making it your day statewide. You served our community very well and it reflects. I remember running around the park during summer camps, events, etc. Everyone would treat me different because of my name. I didn't understand it back then… I understand a little better now. One of my life missions is to help others reach their full potential. Our family has been doing it for a while, even when we were in the Bahamas. I've been doing some research. I have to keep growing and developing. I'm putting everything I have into being the best version of myself. I'm confident it would have a positive effect like you did. Thanks for paving the way.

Grandfathers, I am writing this book because I want to be able to talk to my descendants. I wish I could hear from you from time to time. I can only think about some of the meaningful conversations, insightful knowledge, or wise understandings. I receive so much by listening to others, but the source would have been great. I was inspired to make sure I leave something for my descendants. We are royal. I will not allow them to forget you. I will not allow them to forget me. We must hold each other accountable and to the highest standard. Thank you for embedding so much into my genes and DNA. It was already written before I started. I just had to continue it.

With love and gratitude,
ROYAL DESCENDANT

Dear Nekosha "KO" Chukes,

I miss you more than words can explain. Growing up, you inspired me in so many ways. I remember playing basketball and football. I was always impressed by your ability to compete and beat dudes. I just knew you were going to make it to the NBA. I learned so much from you. I learned different parts of the game from you. Not because you told me, I just paid attention. I grew to be over protective of you. I was willing to put everything on the line for you. I remember the time the huge riot was at EG. It was the time Havana and Gretna fought each other. I was heading out there but y'all already had fought. Reflecting back, I should have been trying to set a better example even though I was younger. Sometimes I should have tried harder to deescalate situations.

I miss the times we would throw parties for the neighborhood. You remember we use to search for the hottest DJ? We knew the crowd would follow the DJ on top of our own fame. My first time getting in the booth was with you. I was nervous for some reason… You weren't listening to me or taking no for an answer. You: "Jay D…" Me: "Get it girl!" Everybody liked the song though. If social media was as hot as it is now, we would've blown up. We were the only ones at our age doing exactly what we were doing back then. We always been generations ahead of ourselves. We've been cooking up some projects and coming together as family though. Ty just shot a music video. She a whole artist now. Dee been staying focused and becoming the best version of himself. He a real go-getter. Tite and I were just at the studio working on some legendary pieces of art. He's been perfecting his craft. We've been networking and building industry connections. We've been working with some award-winning producers. The dream is still alive cousin. I've finally learned how to gain patience. I have been embracing the process of self-growth and personal development. I'm working on developing some more skills too. We're going to surprise you when you come home.

Keep your faith and keep striving to become the best version of yourself. We got it out here. Just continue to build your mind, body, and soul. We are going to the top like we always knew we would. For months, we went a little period without talking because of the car situation. Being out of contact has shown me material value is nothing compared to losing someone you love. Remember, he who angers you controls you. I've learned how to overlook situations, people, and negative energy. I've been working on putting all my energy into positive and productive situations. This was a tough process for me. You know how we came up. But I've learned how to move differently. We have more to lose. We can't allow anyone to trick us from our missions.

*** *Break* ***

After talking to you and hearing you say rap was not your passion anymore made me think… A few lines above, I was expressing my excitement for you to take off when you get out. A voice spoke to me and said you're going to impact and change lives with your story too. Rapping was a vehicle to tell your story vivid. Idk what GOD is calling you to do but the family is with you cousin.

Passionately,
P.J. & JAY D

Dear Jameria "Coby" Conyers,

How you been bro? It's been a minute. I want to say thank you for being a great friend, cousin, and brother. You helped me become tougher playing football, lifting weights, and engaging in the locker room. When we grew up, I never thought either of us would get locked up or fall victim to the system. We all had dreams of making it to the NFL. Life began to happen very fast as we got off to high school. We began to get into different altercations, some of us had kids, and things got a little harder. I just want you to keep your faith brother. We've always been warriors. Learn as much as you can and embrace the process. You're coming home soon. Caleb getting big. I just saw him on Facebook posting like you. I can't believe he's already about to be 6 years old. Time really does fly bro.

I know when your get out you're going to have a very successful come back. Over the years, I've been able to build contacts, resources, and some knowledge. I'm willing to pass and give as much as I can to help you advance at a faster rate. Quin got his CDLs and doing a phenomenal job. He has a whole family now. Nephew grew up fast. Lol, I love you though brother. We're going to win. We will break generational curses. Thank you for believing in me. Thank you for all the times you would push me to keep running, pushing, or going. It's small to some but it was big to me. I'll never forget those moments.

I would also like to apologize for not being there through this process. I still suffer from jail and prison trauma when I use to visit my blood brother and uncles. I was also battling so many things out here that I was not allowed to come visit. There are no valid excuses, I'm not aiming to make any. I'm just letting you know facts along with a sincere apology. Stay strong and understand GOD will not leave nor forsake you. He is only preparing you. Thanks again my brother.

*** Break ***

They always said most of us would not make it. They said we would be a statistic. I never knew how high the odds were stacked against us. We just wanted to have some fun, play ball, and do something others never did. We enjoy our childhood but seem like everything went to falling apart towards the end. Reality of life came crashing down soon as we hit adulthood. We went from everyone about to graduate and head to college to pay ball to injuries, convictions, deaths, separation, fatherhood, etc... I pray for you brother. One day everything will come together and make sense. We didn't struggle for nothing. I remember that time Quan moved to APR in Tallahassee and all of us walked to McDonalds. We put money together to eat good. We split food together, we fought together, and protected each other. I didn't forget about you....

Gratefully,

P.J. & JAY D

Dear Joshua "Big Swole" Green,

What's up brother, we miss you out here. I can't wait for you to come out here to capitalize on the opportunities. I remember you had the vision of becoming a traveling welder when I was still in high school. I didn't see your vision completely. I was still thinking about college degrees. You already knew a trade was going to take off to afford you everything you wanted. I'm seeing it now. Often, I reflect back on many things we did growing up. I think about the parties, conversations, and many other things. I wish we could have gone about doing certain things differently. When you get out, we are going to the top.

Thanks for protecting us all the times you did. Thanks for having everyone back during tough times. Dee Dee moved down South. I see him on social media time to time grinding and doing his thing. Your sisters are holding it down as proud parents. Precious scared me one time, she a strong fighter though. She recovered and bounced back strong. Kaleshia is pushing. She dropped a Jaguar and still has a smile that lights up any room. I'll be glad when you get out bro. It's been a long time, but you still have a long life ahead of you.

I apologize for not being there throughout this entire process. I don't have any excuses. I'm not a man of excuses. Life has really taught me a lot during these years. It will all make sense later. Keep your faith, great energy, and wisdom brother. Learn as much as you can. We are making it through the storm. Remember this family, "Pressure form diamonds". We are brilliantly cut to perfection. Thanks for everything.

*** Break ***

I keep seeing everyone make an honest living from welding. I don't know how much further you have left in your program, but I know it's a winner. I will be a millionaire when you get out. We will be in a position to make things happen. I'm going to send you a copy of this book. I want you to send me some feedback. I feel like we are so old now man. It's so much I know now that I wish I would have known growng up.

Respectfully,

P.J. & JAY D

Dear Kurt Myers,

What's good, we should spar when you get out. I want to see if you still got it. Remember the night we fought in Guthrie Chicken Fingers after the club? I don't even remember why we fought bro. We were so young. They have security and police patrol now. I had fun fighting you. Truth be told, you were my sparring partner. You keep my hands up to date. You were not from Havana, but we could count on you to be there. So much has changed over the years. I'm not a canon anymore. My mindset has shifted in a positive direction. My values have changed. When you get out, we should put on some boxing gloves. Keep your head up and create a plan. Learn as much as you can while you are in there. There are many things out here that needs to be done. Make the time count. One day everything will begin to make since. I often refer to Psalm and Proverbs from the Bible to bring much needed guidance and wisdom. Much love my brother, stay strong.

Genuinely,

JAY D

Dear Michael "Big Mike" Smith,

What's Good G, we miss you cousin. It's been tough out here trying to keep everybody together. I guess we are just getting older. Everybody still cool and can come together but it's different from the old days. Do you remember how we use to come together on Sundays? It's not really like that anymore. Everyone is doing phenomenal though. I'm ready for you to come home. Your little girl is getting big. It still seems like it was just yesterday when she was born. Time is flying cuh… I didn't understand the amount of stress you endured when Ma passed. Initially, you did great coping publicly. Remember, GOD will not give you a burden he didn't equip you to carry. I was looking at an old newspaper article. It was a picture of you and JaQuanice. You talked about how you were raised to respect adults and represent your mother wherever you go. I respect that and you always did represent in a confidently bold way. You have always stood on what you believe. Continue to soak up as much knowledge, wisdom, and understanding possible. You still have a long life to live.

*** Break ***

Love and Loyalty,
P.J. AND JAY D

Dear Uncle "UNC" Harry,

What's up Unc, I miss you OG. I remember coming to your house to sit and talk about life with you. You always told me to keep going and would give me a boost to keep pushing. Uncle Larry came home. I want to see you come home. We had a birthday party at Grandmother's house. I miss Grandma too. Gatherings are still great, but it has not been the same since she left us. I learned so much from you. I learned many principles from you. A man word is his bond. The older I become the more I see why you were usually by yourself or with family. I heard so many stories about you and Uncle Larry growing up. I know the genes got passed down. I've been working on growing and developing into the best version of myself. I wish I would come talk to you about this process. I miss coming to get knowledge and wisdom. I been working on some big projects unc. I've actually disconnected from some friends, family, and loved one. Nobody in our immediate family.

I feel like over the past few years I have been disconnected building a legacy. I need to communicate with you more. I'm going to send you a copy of this book. Write me back and let me know how you like it. I'm going to break some generational curses unc. I was listening to a podcast, audio recording, yesterday and they said it takes at least 100 million to break them for generations. I have a long journey ahead of me but I'm going to make it happen. Our family has poured so much into my growth. I've been able to learn from each and every one of us. Thanks for instilling and showing me as much as you could. I look forward to hearing from you. Much love and respect uncle.

Entirely,
NEPH P.J.

Dear HTTG,

I always knew from the beginning each one of us possessed greatness. Some of us can make a person laugh until they couldn't breathe anymore and tears coming from their eyes… "How ya know fyyyyeeeee" (Smith Vc) Some of could out network a top marketing director. Some of us know how to rap and vividly paint pictures with words. Some of us are deep thinker and can analyze a situation to discover things beneath the surface. Some of us had raw athletic abilities. Some of us had professional fighting skills. There are many more talents individuals possessed but that's for another story. We always been cut from a different cloth. We always had our own style, confidence, and ability to make something out of nothing. Many individuals would not understand the sacrifices made to be here today. Many would not understand the pain we went through when we lost Chad, Trevor, and D. Davis. We suffered major depression, resentful anger, and still learning coping mechanisms to this day. Many would not understand the fights we endured to be allowed into environments. We paved the way for generations after us to have networking opportunities, build relationships, and give them motivation. Each one of us have our own struggles but we have the ability to achieve our goals.

We're still out here making something out of nothing. Most of us grew up in public housing from single parent homes. We're still creating opportunities from thoughts. I saw Quartes, Man Man, last night. This time he was telling the truth. I'm laughing out loud but seriously, he was speaking to Tite, Hitman, about the conversations in the truck. He said, "We use to be laughing and sh*t but PJ use to be saying some real a** sh*t. We just didn't want to hear and thought he used to be tripping. PJ been working and had that same vision." I'm going to be real at first, I thought man was having another moment, but I felt what he was saying… He proceeded to talk about how I influenced some us to go to school when they didn't want to continue. I always saw us being farther and more productive than our immediate surroundings. I never wanted any of us to become a statistic. I always held us to a higher standard. We are not bums, we are not followers, we are not fake, and we are not weak. We are Kings, we are leaders, we are authentic, and we are strong.

My guidance counselors, family members, and other leaders wanted me to separate myself because they believed I was being negatively influenced. Some tried to label me as a gang member. I still don't understand that philosophy. I don't feel like I was being influenced by no more than the media, music, or streets influenced me. I am grateful for the connection we were able to foster. I'm grateful for the brotherhood. I'm grateful for the skills. I'm grateful for the positive accountability. If you look at us now, most of us are productive and striving for greatness. We are not stuck in the same environment. My vision is for us to continue to beat the odds. We cannot let Chad, Trevor, and D Davis names die in vain. We did not come this far to give up.

I rode through the projects the other day and saw Lil CJ. He's grown now. He told me he's a carpenter now. He told me he saw a motivational video I post, and it made him go harder that day. I saw Rod at a store in Tallahassee. He's grown with a family. He told me he's building and stacking. I told him about the book. He told me to keep going... I'm saying this to say... We have to strive for education, personal growth and self-development, socio economic growth, security, professional skill sets, and so forth. We will become multimillionaires and billionaires.

With faith, love, hope and respect,
BROTHER P.J., JAY D., DELEVOE

Dear Vulnerability,

Thank you for allowing me to share parts of my story. My mission is to empower other humans. This has been a challenging but enriching process. Writing has helped shift my emotions, navigate my thoughts, and become self-aware. Pour out my thoughts into this book has helped strengthen me to the core. I didn't complete this book in seven day like Grant Cardone. Nevertheless, the procedure has grown and developed my character. I listened to Brene Brown. She told me to embrace you. Initially, fear began to step in. I went through a series of breakdowns, isolations, and fall outs. I have been so focused on writing this book over the past few months. I've been taking full time express courses while running full-time businesses. I've been transitioning in my businesses. I've even been experiencing some family issues. I will not allow anything to stop me.

My mindset has completely shifted over the last few years. I'm not easily moved or triggered. I've learned how to steadfast in faith and disciplined. I still have a long way to go on this journey. I'm willing to go the extra mile to make a difference. Writing this book has allowed me to go deeper within myself. Writing these letters helped me personally grow past traumas, doubts, and fears. The letters help me commit and find strength within the process. I thought this process was going to be easy. In my mind, I believed I went through the emotions already, so it was a piece of cake writing them.

I've grown to learn our mind and body will relive moments as we reflect them. We will experience the same emotions. I was watching a video on YouTube one day. The video was a test of our brain when we reflect on certain experiences. The stress and anxiety levels of traumas showed during the testing. The human could be in a safe environment, but the thoughts introduced stress and anxiety to the brain. This test helped me understand the importance of handling and releasing issues instead of constantly replaying them over and over. I used to explain stories to my family, friends, or an associate but I was only hurting myself. I was hurting them too because I was spreading negative energy.

I learned to speak life even if I am explaining a "negative" event. Our language shapes our reality. I began to speak from a place of improvement. I learned to have complete faith, hope, and love. My faith has helped me embrace you. I have faith this book will touch and inspire millions to embrace their struggles to unlock their full potentials. I want to see everyone in a winning position. This only way is by healing from the past. I was stuck in my past for so long. I was holding in pain, resentment, and traumas. I was allowing it to hold me down instead of propelling me. I watched Coach Snoop, Snoop Dogg show on Netflix, inspire youth to reach their fullest potential on the football field. Full potentials require discipline, efforts, and commitment. I've often heard the hardest part of accomplishing greatness is beginning. Beginning is the first step towards any great creation. However, many of my hardest times came when I wanted to give up. This is usually the drought before the flood. The athletes, coaches, even parents wanted to give up at times during the show. But Snoop and others inspired them to stay together, push harder, and embrace the process. One episode they flew across the country and lost badly. This helped create their character.

Daring Greatly,
VULNERABILITY PUPIL

Dear Survivors,

I'm so proud of you for not giving up. I'm so proud of you for fighting through it. I'm proud of you more than words can express. You have reasons to quit but you didn't. I'm confident you will go out and do phenomenal things in the world. GOD will not give you a burden he did not equip you to carry. You are already prepared and equipped to handle any obstacles, struggles, or battles. Embrace your struggles to unlock your full potential. In the beginning, it's hard to understand why situations are entering your life. Here's a GEM: *a wise man once said, "And once the storm is over, you won't remember how you made it through, how you managed to survive. You won't even be sure, whether the storm is really over. But one thing is certain. When you come out of the storm, you won't be the same person who walked in. That's what this storm's all about."*

I just want to let you know you are loved. I want to let you know every situation was a blessing not curse. I'm speaking from experience. I'm not speaking out of a book. I'm not speaking from case studies. I'm speaking from pure, raw, and uncensored experiences. I believe life is the best teacher. We often face obstacles, situations, and pain beyond our control. If you're reading this, I want you to regain your power and control. It's okay to not be okay but take advantage of each moment so you can get better. It's okay to say, "No". It's okay to put yourself first. It's okay to fill you cup before pouring into others. When you're on a plane the pilot tells you if the mask falls down during an emergency to put on your mask first. He doesn't tell you to put the mask on the person next to your or behind you. He instructs you to put your mask on first. This is significant because the pilot understands during a state of emergency you have to save yourself first.

In life, sometimes we enter states of emergencies without warning. We are trying to save everyone but ourselves. We are pouring into everyone but ourselves. This letter is to help you declare your state of emergency. This letter is to help you claim your peace. Please do not allow everything you have been through to turn you into a cold person. Choose life over death. I remember when I first thought about writing this book, so many negative thoughts and emotions filled me. I did this for you.

This book is dedicated to anyone who is or has survived struggles, battles, abuse, obstacles, and many other forms of oppression. Embrace the process as Trick Daddy, rapper from Miami's Liberty City, once said, "You gots to hold on, I've been trapped for so long." I know many of you may have felt trapped at some point. It's time to release yourself from mental bondage. Free yourself from the negative, misleading voices in your head. Your past is not your future. You have a phenomenal promised-filled positive life ahead of you. I look forward to reading your letters, emails, and reviews.

Warmest Regards,

PATRICE L. DELEVOE JR.

INSPIRATIONAL TRAUMA SURVIVOR

Dear Community,

Reverend Samuel Delevoe, The Honorable Louis Farrakhan, Marcus Garvey, Patrice Lumba Madam CJ Walker, Malcom X, Muhammad Ali, Nelson Mandela, Cheryl W. Delevoe, Octavious Smith and Tiffany Baker-Smith-Delevoe, Dr. Lois J. Delevoe, Patrice L. Delevoe Sr., Reverend Samuel Delevoe Jr., Dr. Martin Luther King, Jr., Rosa Parks, Sojourner Truth, Attorney Crump, Margret Smith, Jacqueline Wilcoxson, Yolanda Williams, Dr. Cortnie Baity, Tupac Shakur, Patrice Mostepe, Robert Smith, Crystal Jones, Will Stanley, Barrack Obama, Zachary Ansley, Darius Jones, Linda Dilworth, J Anabelle Dias, Ida Walker, Akon, Jamie Johnson, Shawn "Jay-Z" Carter, Tyler Perry, Tony Robbins, Steve Harvey, Will Smith, Prince Donnell, Euro Gotit, Derrick Grace, Mel Gibson, Eric Thomas, Tiphani Montgomery, Toni Morrison, Samuel Paramore, Lisa Nichols, Ray Lewis, Freeway Rick Ross, Jemal King, Nipsey Hustle, Terrence Barber, Keivus Goodson, Johnny House III, Gregory James, Jay Marrison, William Roberts II, Torrence Hatch Jr., Brother Ben X and so forth lead by example, impacted my life and served for the great of our people. Each one of them embraced struggles to unlock their full potential. Each one has contributed to the great of humanity and strengthen my faith in humanity. There's more but I would love to honor and recognize each of these phenomenal individuals.

I have been through many situations. At some point of my life, I was able to look towards your leadership, guidance, and advice to help me. It does take a village. I have not met some of the individuals listed above. Some have passed away. Their works and spirits live on. As we continue to move forward, let's strive to positively influence and strengthen the mindset of the generations to come. The industry music, media, and other outlets of influences are corrupting the minds of our youth. Our youth is our future.

Imagine a garden. Imagine plowing the ground, fertilizing the soil and planting organic seeds in the perfect weather conditions. Every day you nourish the seeds and properly take care of them until you began to see them sprout. The plants began to grow and all of a sudden you start to see weeds, rodents, and insects. Imagine the feelings involved when you take a look at you crop. Think about how fast you would work to remove them from your garden. Now, I want you to think about our community. We are farmers in our community. We have to keep our garden pure and healthy. We have to nourish the environment with positive energy, light and knowledge. Every seed requires a different foundation to reach its full potential. We must take the time out to analyze each other to determine the best environment. We have to enrich the soil with opportunity for exponential growth. We have to prepare for each season, scale our land, and circulate wealth. We have to navigate within our communities like farmers. We have to protect our seeds like farmers.

I just checked my Instagram. Joshua Brown who was a KEY witness in Amber Guyer Murder trial of Botham Jean was murdered. According to Dallas Police there's no suspect. Amber Guyer was a police officer who got sentenced to 10 years. In a powerful speech, Attorney Crump states, "This verdict is for Trayvon Martin, Michael Brown, Sandra Bland, Tamir Rice, Eric Garner, Antwon Rose, Jemel Roberson, EJ Bradford, Stephon Clark, Jeffrey Dennis, Genevive Dawes, Pamela Turner, Philando Castile, Anthony Hill, for so many unarmed black and brown human beings all across America. This verdict is for them."… *Speechless*

Purposefully,
PATRICE L. DELEVOE JR.

Dear Patrice Louis Delevoe Jr.,

I am proud of you. You have been working for years to personal grow and self-defeat. You faced adversity in the face and did not back down. You wrote an entire book while on probation. You lost $16,000 dollars during a break in, then had a Christmas toy and jewelry drive in your hometown. You lost over $100,000+ earned income and found ways to generate $1,000,000 passive income. You battled depression, underwent abuse, fought bullies, dropped out, and still smiled. You never gave up. You struggled but stood tall. You never hated on your homies. In the neighborhood, one would say, "You a good n*gga!" You genuinely care about others. You positively impact others' lives. This may should crazy but I'm proud of being a part of you.

Reflecting over the past generations of your families, I recognize it didn't start with you. It continues with you. It will continue with your kids. It will continue with your supporters. It will continue with your fans. It will continue with generations and generations to come. You're giving them the blueprint, formula, and principles to success. This was your way of documenting it. Although you never got a chance to meet you grandfathers... Even though you lost Chad, Tae Tae, Trevor, D Davis, GODmother Shannon, Bruce and others in the natural form... Alongside Ko, Big Swole, Coby, UNC, Kurt, and many others being incarcerated... You still out here giving out hope, faith, and love. I know they're here with you in spirit. I can feel them as I read your story, hear your voice, or observe your actions.

I am honored to watch you become the best version of yourself. The love you received growing up from your mother, brothers, sister, family members, community, and haters is a reflection of your brilliance. Everyone who comes into contact with you know you are special. It's recognized. Moving forward, I want you to continue keeping GOD first. Embrace your process and stay hungry. When the book is released it's going to change the lives of millions. This book will be talked about in schools, households, and communities. This book will be used to help others. This book is a part of your life calling and story. This book continues our legacy.

I want you to find a phenomenal wife. Find a wife who loves GOD and honor him. Find a wife who will push you to become the best version of yourself. Find a wife who will love you and the family unconditionally. Find a wife who will tough it out with you. Find a woman of virtues. Start a beautiful family and be the best father, grandfather, great father and so forth. Be fulfilled in your marriage. GOD will bring her into your life. She will never leave nor forsake you. Honor her. Love her. Create with her. GOD has been equipping and preparing you.

Write down all your goals, pray over them and become me. I am looking forward to seeing you read this one day. I know you will thank me but until then continue putting in adequate amount of effort. Remember the SBI motto, "No excuse is acceptable, no amount of effort is adequate until proven effective."

Loading,

THE BEST VERSION OF DR. PATRICE L. DELEVOE JR. J.D. G.G

Owner & International Best-Selling Author, Delevoes Lobby LLC

Founder & Millionaire Mentor, Millionaire Mindset Academy

REHABILITATION POEM

Alpha-Bet Guide to a Positive Fulfilling Life

Actions speak louder than words. Be active!

Be a person of understanding. Everyone is on a journey in life.

Create a life worth living. One day you will grow old.

Dedicate your life to becoming the best version of yourself. You deserve it.

Exercise daily. Health is wealth.

Forgive others. Free yourself from your own mental asylum.

Give hope to humanity. A warm heart reflects a kind soul.

Help make the world a better place. Heaven can exist on earth too.

Inspire others. Life or death is in the power of the tongue, speak life.

Join to connect. Experience life without fears, doubts, or uncertainties.

Keep your faith. Success is the sum of efforts repeated daily.

Listen to everyone speak before you talk. Effective communication is important in any relationship.

Motivate individuals around you. Be the change you want to see.

Never give up. Nobody said success would be easy.

Opportunities are endless. Be optimistic!

Pray daily. Problems are inevitable. GODs solutions are plentiful!

Question your intentions. Be loving, righteous and pure!

Reminders hold you accountable for responsibility. Be grateful!

Steps forward represents persistence. Don't give up!

Tears confirm you are still human. Don't change!

Understand instructions and statues. Be resourceful!

Visit the future and pull yourself upward in a positive direction. It's okay to reach, dream big!

Welcome positive thoughts and blessings into your life. Pray daily!

Xerox blueprints. Be inspired to inspire!

Years brings wisdom and understanding. Respect and honor your elders!

Zero excuses. Solutions to problems are effectively…. *incomplete*

REHABILITATION QUOTES

"It's when we start working together that the real healing takes place." – *David Hume*

"As my sufferings mounted, I soon realized that there were two ways in which I could respond to my situation -- either to react with bitterness or seek to transform the suffering into a creative force. I decided to follow the latter course." – *Martin Luther King Jr*

"Hate is self-destructive. If you hate somebody, you're not hurting the person you hate. You're hurting yourself. And that's a healing. Actually, it's a real healing, forgiveness." – *Louis Zamperini*

"Any psychologist will tell you that healing comes from honest confrontation with our injury or with our past. Whatever that thing is that has hurt us or traumatized us, until we face it head on, we will have issues moving forward in a healthy way." – *Nate Parker*

"Love one another and help others to rise to the higher levels, simply by pouring out love. Love is infectious and the greatest healing energy." – *Sai Baba*

"GOD put me on this earth to bring souls back to the Kingdom of GOD. You don't need to pray ten times a day - you just need hope. My music is going to stop war; it's the healing music. I see myself in Brazil, in Syria, in Darfur, and places where they really need hope." – *Tory Lanez*

"Physicians need to be good technicians and know how to prescribe, but for healing to occur, they also need to incorporate philosophy and spirituality into their treatment. We need to feel as well as think." – *Bernie Siegel*

"Those are the same stars, and that is the same moon, that look down upon your brothers and sisters, and which they see as they look up to them, though they are ever so far away from us, and each other." – *Sojourner Truth*

"I freed thousands of slaves. I could have freed thousands more if they had known they were slaves." – *Harriet Tubman*

"The most common way people give up their power is by thinking they don't have any." – *Alice Walker*

"The moment we choose to love we begin to move against domination, against oppression. The moment we choose to love we begin to move towards freedom, to act in ways that liberate ourselves and others." – *Bell hooks*

"Sometimes you've got to let everything go- purge yourself. If you are unhappy with anything… whatever is bringing you down, get rid of it. Because you'll find that when you're free, your creativity, your true self comes out." – *Tina Turner*

PRECIOUS ARTIFACT

Discovered on March 12, 2019 from Facebook Broward County Black Owned Businesses Group

#BrowardCounty #BlackHistory #DIDYOUKNOW series:

Black Love, Activism, and Tragedy

THE STORY OF REVEREND SAMUEL J. DELEVOE AND DR. LOIS J. DELEVOE

Samuel Delevoe was born March 04, 1936, his family moved to Liberia when he was a child, in Liberia he attended Attucks. In his teenage years, Delevoe joined the Korean War then went back to Dillard to finish high school. Samuel fell in love and married Lois Delevoe in 1959, she describes him as a loving family man and as a provider. Samuel Delevoe became one of the first black police officers in Fort Lauderdale and vowed to bridge the gap between the black community and the police force. Through being a community advocate, Delevoe became the president of a contracting group called "Broward county minority builders" president of the black coalition of Broward county, got involved in real estate, a member of HOPE and was one of the main organizers that brought peace to the community dissolving several conflicts during the riots in Fort Lauderdale. In 1968, Samuel Delevoe became a street minister who also focused more on his entrepreneurship. Many people younger than him looked towards him for guidance and motivation, he would help people out who were going through rough times economically. Talking about Samuel Delevoe, we must always acknowledge Lois Delevoe who was also a thriving entrepreneur herself. She was the first black woman in Broward county to open up a black credit union, started "clean sweep" which was a community clean up that brought together cooperation between city officials, black business owners, international entertainers like James Brown and the community itself, owned a thrift shop, also opened up a facility to accommodate several people who were homeless. The facility had a cafeteria, child care and space for counseling. Dr. Delevoe even ran for the Florida house in 1972 and the Broward county commission in 1976. In 1977, tragedy struck when an irate yardman went into the real estate office Samuel Delevoe was in, a confrontation broke out due to the yardman stealing from Mr. Delevoe. Samuel and Lois Delevoe were both shot. Lois was shot in the arm, but Samuel's wound ended up killing him. She stood in the streets for 10 minutes screaming for help. The Delevoes had 2 sons and the city of Fort Lauderdale honored him by naming "Samuel Delevoe park" after him. Lois Delevoe has still been active by teaching in the Dade and Broward county school systems and even taught at a few of the south Florida colleges and worked in conjunction with Broward county parks and recs. The Delevoes have made their mark as one of the premier families of Black Broward through their contributions to their community through community development and economic growth. #Black-Broward #BHM954 #Lauderdale info provided Emmanuel George

STOP ARMAGEDDON

Poem created by Patrice Delevoe
in 2012 during AP Literature Class

Stupidity

over-flowing our nation, hate over race and
we're all adjacent

Tension

anger, animosity, attitude built
kkk emerge, many killed

Ops

biggest mistake, hatred
fuel on fire, open death gates

Privation

filled many home, but money comes to the ground which
is home of poor and land of the rich

America, America

Home of the free, Land of the brave,
United, as, one, yet many slaves

Rage

labor in southern state, no pay
in the rivers, ancestors wade.

Misery

disparity, poverty soaks the land
children victimized, never given chance

Alteration

seeds planted, less cotton in the fields
more opportunities, MLK killed

Gullible

lied to, betrayed
back on the walls, no help, no faith

Earthquake

everyone rumbled, cries over looked
pause - civil movement fumble

Depression

bright light darkens, endless battle being fought
don't give up, peace will be sought

Development

seeds grow, opinions change
plants recognized, change in the game

Oppression

no longer a factor,
but justice served, Thurgood Marshall heard

Novelty

one day shall come.
United, States, of America

UNITED-AS-ONE

6

SELF-EXAMINATION

A WISE UNPOPULAR GREEK PHILOSOPHER named Socrates once proclaimed, "The unexamined life is not worth living." After consciously examining my authentic existence, my true identity began to uncover. I watched a snippet of the 2019 B.E.T awards, honoring African-American excellence and extraordinary achievements. Tyler Perry, a former homeless self-made multimillionaire, connected passionately with millions of viewers explaining the process of manifesting his success. He emphasized the importance of owning your stuff. Owning your stuff wholeheartedly is the true essence of self-examination. In retrospect, self-examinations helped me identify the power of an enriched foundation, purposeful transformation, personal growth, and self-development. Self-examinations helped me embrace the power of inspirational traumas, cooperative triumphs, and breech birthed philosophies. My childhood, adolescence, and early stages of adulthood examination has confirmed my life is worth living.

I advise all readers to set aside time to examine yourself. I'm confident you will find purposeful reasons to live. In an influential society, a human can easily be misled or guided to neglect their true essence. I once read, "Every man has two educations, that which is given to him and that which he gives himself." This philosophy will serve as a supporting pillar during my self-examination to identify how power is gained from an enriched foundation. I define education as knowledge, wisdom, and understanding from but not limited to personal experiences, traditions lessons, or institutional teachings. Education was given to me through many forms.

My character is a product of my education. I was born without conscious knowledge of behaviors. I was born without life wisdoms. I was born without understanding due to lack of experiences. I believe my education set a foundation of excellence, produced life changing experiences, created survivor instincts, and established a positive tone for my life. This belief is supported by a self-examination of four stages of human development. Throughout this chapter, I will examine each stage based on factual sources, brief analysis, and experiences.

After examining my Infancy/Toddler pictures, I recognize a bright smile, uplifting spirit, and determination. I kept a smile on my face in and the during traumatic or unfortunate experiences. For example, one night my oldest brother Larry forgot a pot of grease was heating up. My mother and I was in the room until we began to smell smoke and hear popcorn like sounds. I immediately ran outside across the street to Ms. Pookie apartment, she was a family friend. Everyone came outside. My mother panicked as she came outside of our apartment. She thought I was still in the house. I was only about three or four years old, but I smiled and hugged her. I was not sad. I was happy that both of us were safe. I was not worried about the apartment. Wow, I just realized that was a part of my experience growing up. We lost so much in that fire. I never cared about losing things because GOD always provided a way to get them back plus more.

Here's another example, my father, brother E.T. and I were on the way back from Fort Lauderdale, Florida. I noticed my dad anxiety began to increase as we traveled back home. A couple hundred miles away from home, the station wagon began to have mechanical issues. I smiled and told my dad not to worry, everything will work out. We walked on the side of the interstate that evening. I laughed and joked while everyone was irritable. Sometimes during conversing, my dad reminds me of this funny story.

My mother and father laughed while telling me, "You tried to run before you walked." I would get enough balance on two feet then run as many steps as I could before landing on my bottom. This behavior began to reflect in everyday life. I would run to start projects. I didn't care about failing because I knew how to get up to try again. Sometimes, you have to bust your behind to get ahead. This continued through my life. I quickly observed that some of life's best lessons come from experiences. Often, I would fall but each lesson from the drop has only intensified my hunger. My examination was based on pictures, family stories, and pieces of memory. Self-examinations and reflections help us remember and establish the foundations of our identities.

After examining my childhood, I recognized habits to dominate, excel expeditiously, serve GOD, and lead. I built habits to think critically, find solutions promptly, openly express honest thoughts, and develop creativity. On the other hand, I recognized habits to protect my unbalanced emotions, openly express my anger, allow my negative thought to control me, and my perfectionism. I included "my" because I wanted to make sure I took ownership of each one. My examination was based on tucked away memories, academic and athletic awards, reflective conversations, pictures, and other credible sources. In the fifth grade, I became upset for weeks at my gifted teacher for a B on my report card. I had all As. This was the first time I would have every earned all As. I was so happy until I saw my last grade. I allowed one letter to take away from my other hard work. However, it pushed me to work harder, smarter, and taught me communication skills. I graduated the second in my class at Gadsden Elementary Magnet School, GEMS. Here's A GEM: *Get smarter by educating yourself.* Don't settle for average because it's easily attainable.

Here's some priceless advice to parents, guardians, and so forth. Put your child into a nourishing educational environment. In my ignorance, I believe the first stages of human development establishes their abilities to think properly, function on an optimized level, and produce the driving force behind their actions. In the Holy Bible, Proverbs Chapter 22 verse 6 drops a GEM: *Train up a child in the way he should go: and when he is old, he will not depart from it.* I'm a believer of the Word. I am a living testimony. I drifted away multiple times due to many influences throughout my adolescence.

After examining my adolescent, I observed learned habits to impress others, gain recognition, demand for respect, and an increased desire for love/belonging. According to an article published by Saul McLeod on simplypsychology.org, Maslow Hierarchy is a motivational theory in psychology comprising a five-tier model of human needs, often depicted as hierarchical levels within a pyramid. Needs lower down in the hierarchy must be satisfied before individuals can attend to needs higher up. From the bottom of the hierarchy upwards, the needs are: physiological, safety, love and belonging, esteem and self-actualization. Based on the Maslow Hierarchy of needs, I recognized my needs shifted throughout grade school. I was not recognized as a star student anymore. I lost self-esteem. My circle of friends seemed to decrease as grade levels increased. I didn't feel like I belonged in many of my social environments. I didn't have a strong relationship with my father. This created a void in my heart. Subconsciously, I felt like I needed love. I embraced and used relationships as a crutch. I turned to the streets for notoriety. I began to feel disconnected from my old identities as I gained new ones. I had over four alias and each came with a specific personality.

During my adolescence, I had to learn how to be confident outside of academic environments. I developed social skills in uncomfortable environments. I discovered the power of networking to achieve objectives. I was exposed to fast money opportunities and impactful connections. I was arrested for the first time. I was protected from death on multiple occasions. My adolescents were filled and shaped by phenomenal individuals, wisdom birthed experiences, and priceless lifelong lessons. This was an intense and heated period in my life. Here's a GEM: *Find yourself and never lose yourself.*

To all my young brothers and sisters, strive for greatness without doubts, fears and uncertainties. Do not allow fear or pride to stop you from finding help. Be as resourceful as possible. Find a mentor, guidance counselor, and information. I know many of you want to be independent and do things on your own. Trust me, your time will come. There's no shortcut to success so you will have your fair share of responsibilities, obligations, and commitments. Enjoy your youthful years. Do not rush into anything that's not going to add value to you. Do not allow others to influence you to do something that's going to risk your freedom, reputation, or livelihood. Keep your head up. Be sure of yourself and trust the process. Question others motives and do your own research. Steadfast in faith and keep GOD first.

On the journey towards my personal legend, I've experience mental, physical, and spiritual shifts. I have personally grown and self-develop. Oprah Winfrey once said, "Failure is GOD's way of saying excuse me, you're going in the wrong direction." My greatest growth has come from many failures. I was willing to fail to become successful. I failed to finish college. I failed to defeat depression during our first battles. I failed to succeed in my cooking business. I failed to manage funds properly. I failed many intimate and personal relationships. I have failed countless times. The failures helped me develop a hunger and deeper appreciation for success.

During the process, something happens between the start and finish. I experienced inspirational traumas. I experienced life changing experiences. I experienced multiple phenomena. I experienced buildups and setbacks. I experienced cooperative victories. I experienced reflective moments. I experienced life. I suffered but I gain so much. I gained an appreciation for the small things in life. I gained a sense of gratitude. I gained a positive identity. I gained the ability to make decisions. I gained the Millionaires Mindset. I gained access to resources. I gained a strong connection and relationship with GOD.

After examining my young adulthood, I observed learned behaviors to contribute positively to society, inspire others, commit to personal growth and self-development, become financial free, and educate others. I recognized that I am still growing and developing into the best version of myself. I am not perfect. I still make mistakes. I still fail. I still cry. I still struggle. However, I am improving. I am committed to become the best version of myself. I talk to myself in the mirror from an older successful state. I allow the best version of myself to mentor struggling parts of me. I have grown. These claims are based on videos, pictures, awards, recognitions, and current work ethics. I'm honored to write a truthful transformation memoir about my journey.

My self-examinations have led me to provide additional words of wisdom, encouragement, and motivation. In the heights of success, I was on a flight from Miami, Florida heading to Atlanta, Georgia for a life changing opportunity. The pilot warned us. He let us know, "we will be experiencing some turbulence." I heard him through my ears, but my soul received a message. This was a reminder even throughout the highest moments you can run into obstacles. The obstacles are only obstacles. If you're running a marathon, you simply figure out the most efficient way to get past the obstacles. If you're flying a plane, you simply buckle up and fly through it.

One of my life missions is to help everyone reach their full potential. I will do this by passing forward my education. Some of you may have heard this before and some of you may be hearing it for the first time. Remember, knowledge without application is similar to faith without work. It's necessary to apply this knowledge. It's necessary to digest this information. It's necessary to try. One of my brothers, Bryant Finley, has a famous quote. He inquisitively asks, "How you gone be a G.O.A.T if you don't Go Out And Try?". In life, you must try if you want to succeed. Do not be afraid of failure. It's a part of the process. When learning to walk, as I mentioned earlier, I bust my behind multiple times. I can walk miles now. I used to fall after a few steps.

As entrepreneurs, we have to capitalize and monetize resources while adding as much value as possible. We have to turn our network into net-worth. We are living in an age where social media thrives. We have the ability to connect and explore like never before. We have access to seminars, webinars, valuable information, and so forth. As we connect, we must always deliver more than what's expected. Showing genuine love, respect, and professional ethics. Using these formulas allowed me to break away from negative stereotypes and empowered me to make a living in the business word. I'm confident they will do the same for each and every one of you.

As an investor, we are investing to gain positive returns. Adolph Thornton, Jr., widely known as Young Dolph, is a successful rap artist from Memphis, Tennessee. On his single, "Get Paid" Young Dolph gives investors rules from his experience. During his lectures, he states, "Rule number 1, get the money first! Rule number 2, don't forget to get the money! Play by these rules and everything will be okay!" I agree with his rules. Make sure you get the money when you close a deal. Make sure you have your numbers together before closing a deal. Make sure everyone is extremely happy and make an informed decision.

As generational wealth builders, it's very important to create passive streams of income. The average millionaire has seven sources of income. I did not say seven jobs. Seven sources of income. This means we allow money to work for us instead of us working for money. We save at least 10-15 % of our earnings. These principles from Rich Dad, Poor Dad by Robert Kiyosaki never left my brain. It has always stuck with me. When you make your business model, keep this in mind. As a matter of fact, make sure you read the book for yourself. Learn from him. Watch his videos on YouTube. Attend his workshops and seminar while you have time. He is a pillar of the financial literacy community. Thank you, Rich Dad and Robert Kiyosaki.

As a real estate investor, remember the Monopoly rule. Get three green houses and a red hotel. Continue repeating this process until you reach your goals. Many successful real estate gurus refer to this rule. Jemal King, @9to5millionaire, shared his knowledge at Eric Thomas 1% event. He started his journey early. He became a police officer in Chicago but still made time to become a real estate investor.

He's a living testimony that this system works. I advise everyone to connect with him and discover the gems he has to offer.

As a royal descendant, create a positive legacy for your family, friends, loved ones, and future generations to come. I never meet my Grandfathers. However, their legacies are able to live through me. This book will serve as a way to connect future generations to come. Make sure you take the time out to create a will, blueprint, and foundations. When you understand you come from greatness, it becomes easier to tap into your greatness.

As leaders, we must become the best version of ourselves, everything else will increase. To become the best version of yourself you must be committed. Merriam-Webster definition of commitment is an agreement or pledge to do something in the future. If you agree to become the best version of yourself, you are agreeing to learn positive habits, personal grow and self-develop, spread light throughout humanity, and contribute positively to your community. In my opinion, the best way to make progress is by aligning your mind, body, and soul.

As a student, trust the process. Everything will align and come together in due time. Through my journey, I've been there and there are no shortcuts. You can't cut corners, but you can personally grow and self-develop into a better version of yourself. The more value you add to yourself the more valuable you will be to anything around you. Wealth is a reflection of the value you add to the world. Millionaires and Billionaires are wealthy because of the value their companies add to society. Here's a GEM: *Become a giver and you will receive.*

As a winner, do not allow pride, ego, and success to take away your humility. I believe GOD will take it away as fast as you receive it. I believe in staying humble. Celebrate your victory but do not look down on others. Treat others how you want to be treated. Be the energy you want to receive. The Law of Attraction has shown me on multiple occasions that you get what you put out into the universe. My mother taught me at a young age to treat others how you want to be treated.

Here's a GEM: *Run towards the truth*. Embrace your identity. If you don't like your identity, make changes to become the best version of yourself. Imagine being the best version of yourself. Ask yourself a question, "Will I be in this situation if I was the best version of myself?" If the answer is no, then you have to changes to make to your life. Remember, you are not your situation. The elders in our community always said, "The truth will set you free." I believe the truth will set you free. In my ignorance, living a lie is very challenging and uncomfortable. Be truthful with yourself. It's important to live inside of yourself. Don't change because you want somebody else to appreciate you more. Love yourself and stop allowing insecure people to place their insecurities on you.

ENCOURAGEMENT

The Dreamer and Doer

Focus on your dreams, studies, and aspirations. This is a phenomenal time to be alive. Use all your resources to add value to your mission. Stay encouraged while you build your dreams. Focus on becoming a better you. As you become the best version of yours, everyone will not understand. Many leaders are misunderstood in the beginning. Study the books and apply the knowledge. Trust the process. GOD will send you the right individuals needed to help you build. Do not force anything. Remember, an individual is adding or subtracting from you. Surround yourself around a team who wants to see you win. It's challenging manifesting dreams. It's challenging doing the work. Be encouraged with positive vibrations and high frequencies. GOD bless you on your journey. May you have an overflow of blessings, protection, happiness, peace, and prosperity.

The Beggar

Stop asking everyone for help and help yourself. Find some resources. Go to the public library and read self-help books. Personal growth and self-development books will help mentally prepare you. Inspirational books will give you some fuel when you feel like giving up. Financial literacy books will help you know what to do with your money when you get it. Emotional intelligent books will help you gain power and control over your feelings. If you're really committed, sign up for the Millionaires Mindset Academy. Seek out a coach and mentor. Accountability is everything. Let someone hold you accountable and reach for success without being dependent. Everything you need is already inside of you.

The Thief

Everything comes with a price. The price can be your life, freedom, or other forms of payments. I've watched in many circumstances the results of taking without permission. This blessed me with the wisdom to make smart decisions. Sometimes you get away, but you cannot escape the laws of the universe. Things will catch up to you when you're least expecting it. Please be mindful of the company you keep. They can influence you to make negative decisions. You can be guilty by association. A wise man once said, "You show me your friends and I'll show you who you are." If you hang with thieves then nine times out of ten, you are one or will become one. Additionally, I believe in Karma. I've seen Karma happen in many forms. Karma has happened to me. Karma has helped individuals around me. It usually comes when you least expect it. Be mindful of the things you do to others. A person will hurt or kill you about their hard-earned possession. Before you think about taking something from someone, please reflect on this reading. My mission is to help save your life. I've lost friends to similar situations.

The Misfit

Did you know the 1% is different from 99% of the world? Did you know the 1% accounts for 40% of the nation's wealth? The 1% are not focused on fitting in because they're too busy standing out. Stop trying to force yourself to settle for positions. Stop trying to fit into place that are not for you. Be your true and authentic self. Allow your energy to radiate. You are phenomenal. You are enough. You have greatness within you. You have endless capabilities. Make sure you strive to become the best version of yourself. Unlock your full potential. Make sure you do what's necessary to reach the next levels of your success. Write the book. Take the test. Study the greats. Make the change. Be the inspiration to inspire a nation. Do not settle for average. You've never been average so don't start being average now. I love you. I am you. We are misfits.

The Star

How to get focus? Cut off all your electronics. Yes, your cellphone and television. You have to take control to get where you need to be. If you are determined to succeed, then you need to stop scrolling your screen. It's time to plan your life. Take an assessment of the five individuals closest to you. In all your relationships there are two things happening, someone is adding or subtracting from you. Be honest with yourself. Are the five people closest to you adding or subtracting from you? Make sure each move you make is purposeful. Make sure you live with purpose on purpose. Believe in yourself. A key formula from The Secret is Ask, Believe, and Receive. This formula is also used in the Holy Bible. Once you ask for something live as if it's already on the way to you. Here's a GEM: *You can't pray and worry at the same time.* If you want natural phenomena to happen in your life, you have to stay focused. Keep your eyes on the prize and believe in the vision. GOD gifted you the vision for a reason. It's going to come to fruition. You can work towards something for four year to have a major breakthrough in the fifth. Keep your faith. Don't allow your light to be dimmed. Allow your light to shine unapologetically. Light up every room you enter and be the burst of energy you want to receive.

The Gambler

If you're familiar with playing card games. Imagine receiving a hand from the dealer. If you receive a hand you do not like It's not your fault. However, it's your responsibility to embrace it to your full potential. You play them to the best of your ability. If you keep a straight face, smile, and play them right, you usually do better than anticipated. The game itself is all about strategy. Don't get stuck into suffering. Suffering throws you off your game. All perform at the top of your game. You may get a better hand next time. In the game of spades, sometime your partner has a better hand. I recognized GOD as my partner. I trust GOD enough to know he has the upper hand. He has all the cards needed to win the game. I just have to keep trusting him as I play the game. I would encourage you to become a master in Chess. Card games are very nice and fun. Chess requires deeper thinking and more strategy. Exercise your brain with some chess games. It will help you find a great balance between fast moves and slow calculated moves. I believe in calculated risk. I don't believe in all out gambling. I trust that you will understand the difference between the two.

The Perfectionist

During an interview published on YouTube, Will Smith said, "Lay each brick perfectly." He was describing the way a brick mason creates a building. This is similar to the concept, starting small. As I listened to Will Smith, I could not help but reflect on the time I opened four business without understanding the small details of each one. I tried to build so fast that everything fell apart almost overnight. The key is to building a foundation is precision, blueprints, and consistency. Yes, it may take longer. Yes, you may get frustrated. Yes, you will feel like giving up. However, keep your faith and remember why you started. Get focused on laying the bricks. Don't focus on the buildings around you. Don't focus on the time for the project. Focus on the task at hand. Do you best and your skills will sharpen along the way. I remember sometimes I would want things to be so perfect that it keeps me from starting. Initially, that was the problem with writing this book. I wanted it to be perfect. However, most of natural diamonds have inclusion and blemishes. Don't allow being perfect cause you to procrastinate. I believe in you. I know you will do what's required to leave a legacy for generations to come.

The Neighborhood Negus

When I started this book, I was on probation. Yes, Mr. Successful CEO and Motivator with a Department of Correction number. I wanted everybody to know how the system was against me. I wanted everyone to know how I didn't do anything wrong. I was led by frustrations. I was followed by shame. I am a real hustler with a heart of gold. How can this happen to me? I was not selling drugs… I was not breaking into houses… I was not robbing or hurting anybody… I was just trying to make an honest living… I was getting blown away in my storm. My storm was affecting everyone close to me. I was raining negative energy on everyone. I was not doing this intentionally. However, my energy was draining to me and everyone around me.

I began to feel like nobody cared about me and my situation. I felt like I gave everyone the world and they didn't give me back nothing. I felt like it was messed up that some people didn't even take the time to connect with me. I could go on and on about my feelings but that's going to be in the next series. Here's the truth: I messed up. I made a mistake from being ignorant. Once I accepted my responsibility, I was able to birth this book. This was the first time in years that I was stationary. I took advantage of the time to get ahead in other areas of my life. Life is about making the most out of every situation. This is possible with a positive mindset. Keep the negative out so the positive can have room to enter.

BREECH BIRTHED PHILOSOPHIES

The Diamond

Often, we aim to become without understanding the process of becoming. In my ignorance, before a natural diamond is formed it starts deep within the ground. The natural diamond is surrounded by darkness. The natural diamond has intense pressure molding it from all directions. The temperatures are extremely high. A natural diamond endures these conditions for an extended period of time. The formation of a diamond is not an "overnight" process. Natural diamonds are not "overnight" creations. Natural diamonds form into many different shapes, sizes, and colors. Once the diamond emerges and is discovered, it's cut and polished before it's displayed. After this process the diamond is graded. Based on GIA Diamond Grading Scale, the diamond is graded based on the cut, color, clarity, and carat weight. This is formally known as the 4Cs.

Synthetic diamonds are perfectly created in laboratories. The right conditions help these diamonds form very quickly. They come out perfect without inclusions, blemishes, and other flaws natural diamonds possess. Synthetic diamonds look beautiful. They appear as high clarity natural diamonds. Some individuals love them. Many prestigious individuals despise them. Synthetic diamonds are much cheaper and more affordable. A person can easily gain access to a high volume of them.

Although the synthetic diamonds are beautiful, they are not highly valued in the market of precious gemstone. They have the same chemical composition. They share a brilliant luster and can be colored. They can be perfectly cut. However, the process is different. The process the natural process undergo is rare. The process increases the value. The process makes a natural diamond with blemishes, inclusion, and flaws worth more than a flawless synthetic diamond. Here's a GEM: *The process adds value.* I took this philosophy and adopted it. I would rather go through the natural process to become a natural diamond.

The Eagle

I've always heard the quote, "Change your attitude, change your altitude.". My teachers would use this quote to help me understand the power of my attitude. When I was younger, I would vividly express my emotions. I would knock stuff over, hit walls, breathe intensely, and fight anyone who bothered me. I was a loose cannon. I had the wrong attitude. Once I changed my attitude, my life began to change. I began to get along with individuals. I began to make better connections. I began to rise. The rise was my altitude. In elementary school, I rose to the top of my class before our graduation. This was a great accomplishment for someone who struggled to get along with students initially. I committed to staying at the top. I began to love the feeling of flying high. I loved the challenges that came with achieving great accomplishments. I wanted to soar. As I grew older, I began to cross paths with like-minded individuals. Over the past few years, I've adopted the Eagle as my spirit animal.

I have some fast facts about the eagle. If an eagle sees another bird in its path during flight, it has to be another eagle. Other birds do not fly as high as the eagle. This touched my soul because I began to feel loneliness achieved high levels of success. I felt like I couldn't share it with anyone, because they would not be able to understand some of the challenges I face. I felt like I couldn't share because everyone would have their hand out. I recognized; I began to soar alone. I planned trips to conference to connect with other eagles. They understood.

Dr. Myles Munroe explains that an eagle is the only bird that loves the storm. The eagle uses the winds of the storm to rise and is pushed higher. The eagle uses the pressure of furious airstream to soar. The wind is also used to clean debris from the eagle wings. Frequently, we face storm throughout our journey. I've adapted the spirit of the eagle. I challenge you to adapt the spirit of the eagle.

The Lion

Courage comes from a French word, of the heart. Your heart is the driving force behind your actions. I showed Floyd Mayweather, undefeated professional boxer, a picture of this book cover before it was completed. He smiled as I explained to him what and why I wrote it. We locked hands in brotherhood. We unified and congratulated each other. We come from humble beginnings. We struggled to reach our full potential. We're beating the odds. A champion stands shoulder back, head up, and stare adversity in the eyes without fears, doubts, or uncertainties. Champions focus on the objective despite the noise from the opposition or the sideline. We have been showing the world what champions look like.

I must be completely honest. I did not know what to expect from him. Upon his arrival, I had only seen him box and post on social media. Inside of the Moon nightclub, he was a gentleman. He shook hands while looking you directly in the eye. He gave words of encouragement and wisdom. He was a stand-up guy. He didn't come off as arrogant or belligerent. I was actually surprised. He was a gentleman.

As he stood tall in spirit, I observed his size. Mayweather was not the largest. He was not the strongest. He is still undefeated. He is the world champion. How? His actions have shown, Floyd Mayweather has heart. He's similar to a Lion roaming in Sub-Saharan Africa. He protects his territory. He does not possess fear. He is brave and courageous. His heart grants him the ability to dominate. His heart gives him the courage to defend the title. I believe everybody that we meet is going to be for a reason to help serve a purpose. When I meet him, I received a boost of energy to keep pushing. He flew into town on his private jet for a couple hours to shake hands, smile and motivate others. I am confident I will do the same later on my journey. Thank you, Floyd Mayweather, for the boost.

This leaves me with a message for anyone who struggle being brave or courageous. When the bullies of life try to knock you down, you stick and move. Take a jab at it like Mayweather. If you choose to do something, kick the door open and attack the objective. Remember, every day is a hunt. A lion hunts daily because it has to provide for its family. A lion does what it necessary to survive. I've adopted the spirit of the lion. I challenge you to adopt this spirit.

The Royal Descendant

As royal descendants, we know we are Kings and Queens. We have to inherit the habits of the royal. We are not beggars. We do not settle. We are not weak. We are not followers. We are lenders, not borrowers. We are a part of the Kingdom. We are connected to the source. We are internally fulfilled. We understand everything we need is inside of us. We are filled with knowledge, wisdom, and understanding. We do not complain. We do not possess fear. We lead our village to the promised land. We do exceedingly and abundantly well. We set high standards.

We honor our bodies as temples. We protect our spirits. We do not allow the enemy to manipulate us. We stick together as one. We treat each other with the utmost respect. We are grateful for everything. We are kind. We are bold. We are the change. We have faith. We give hope. We produce love. We set examples. We create generational wealth. We build legacies. As a royal descendant there's much required because much was given.

It's your birthright to lead so surround yourself with people who are on the same mission as you. Dr. Myles Munroe said, "You can have potential but if you don't have the belief then your potential becomes a victim of your present belief." Look at yourself in the mirror and address yourself as a royal descendant. I declare a shift in your belief system. I declare an increase in your faith, hope, and love. May your life abundantly overflow in wealth, peace, serenity, fulfillment, strength, resources, and protection. GOD bless you. I am inheriting my birthright. I challenge you to inherit yours.

The Scholar

During an interview Jay Z made a strong point when he said, "Who's better to coach the people than someone who played the game." I've begun coaching, educating, and mentoring others. I believe each one should teach one. We have to hold each other accountable and share responsibility. How can one speak of community love without a standard? I believe as Kings and Queens we should share our experiences, resources, and gifts with each other. I recognize many individuals don't know how to improve. I listened to the Secret by Rhonda Byrne. This book helped me gain a positive mindset. It also increased my hunger for personal growth and self-development. I played the game of negativity for so long. I played the game of poverty for so long. I even played the game of being a victim for so long.

After committing to Millionaires Mindset Academy, I became a coach. I helped leaders take their game to the next level. I changed negatives to positives. I changed poverty thinking to abundance thinking. I have helped trauma victims heal and become survivors. I was not only enhancing myself, but I was improving a community. My commitment impacted the individuals around me. Positive energy is contagious. Sharing knowledge and information became a hobby. Occasionally, I wonder if I should share my thoughts or beliefs. I always ask GOD to allow me to be a vessel of him.

As I continued this journey, the spirit of GOD grew. I believe I am a spirit with a body, not a body with a spirit. I've been working to become less of my flesh so I can ascend my spirit. I believe our realities exist in multiple realms, heavens and earth. In my opinion, the less time we spend focused on earthly possession, the more time we can spend in the heavens. The more time we can spend in the heavens, the more time we have to connect with GOD. We have the power to connect the dots by aligning our mind, body, and soul. My experiences have shaped my beliefs. I've seen my dreams and dream enter my physical realm. I've mediated on things that appeared a few months later. My dreams are more vivid. My mediations are guided. I have grown to love nature like never before. I adopted the belief of being a student of life. I challenge you to become a student of life.

REFLECTIONS

Enriched foundation was great reflections over my life. I gained a deep sense of appreciation for the individuals who pour so much into my growth and development. I was not always calm and collected. I did not always see thinking from positive lens. I'm so grateful for each person who took the time out to be patience, caring, and optimistic. I learned that everyone has greatness within, but it takes the right energy to bring it out of them.

Personal growth and self-development showed me I had to go through great suffering to gain knowledge, wisdom, and understanding. As I wrote this chapter, I was astonished at the dedication, drive, and determination to keep going. I changed my perspective. I saw the cup as half full instead of half empty. I advise everyone reading to reflect over their perspectives. See the cup as half full. Pour into mind, body, and spirit until your cup overflows.

Inspirational traumas helped me understand how I remained in a dark place for so long. I was so disappointed in myself. However, I am inspired by my strength. I caught chills reading my story. The first time reading the therapy sessions manuscript pointed out a hurt I never openly expressed. I was quite about my pain. I would vent on Facebook from time to time. But anytime someone saw me, I would have a smile on my face. I was deeply hurting instead despite life achievements.

Collective Triumphs was defining moments in my life. I come from a tough environment. Love is occasionally shown within my neighborhood, but it was a dog eat dog world. When I started the business, I carried a negative notion about community support. Outside of my immediate family and loved ones, I thought I had to do everything on my own. I received so much love and help from everyone. My investors became my family. My clients became my family. My community became my family. We won collectively. We turned traumas to triumphs.

Rehabilitation took the longest to write. I ran from this chapter subconsciously. Most of the struggles were easily addressed when I decided to address them. I believe the toughest part of any struggle, addiction, dysfunction, and so forth is acknowledgement. The lack of acknowledgement leave room for the problem to go untreated and unsolved. I took a break when I wrote everyone name down. I almost became depressed again. I always heard letters are great for releasing emotions. I let my emotions out. I used to write letters on social media about my issues when I was younger, unpolished, and a little rougher around the edges. It served as a temporary release but generated additional problems. This time I poured it all into an inspirational, empowering book.

Last but not least, this chapter was a deeper look. Each stage of my life has been driven by some sort of purpose. I just had to analyze the events, memories, and embrace them. I am inspired to inspire. I really enjoyed this chapter because I was directly able to pass lessons forward. Reflecting over the experiences writing this book has been uplifting. Almost 75,000 words later, I completed my mission. I stuck it out. I didn't give up. I didn't complete the book within 7 day like Grant Cardone, but I did complete it. I completed the book within 6 months. I completed the book while completing probation. I completed the book while running a business full time. I completed the book as a full-time student. I completed the book while being completely active in my family. I completed the book while becoming the best version of myself. This is one of my greatest accomplishments. I know this book is going to help so many individuals become the best version of themselves. I know this book is going to help others embrace their struggles to unlock their full potential.

MOVING FORWARD

As a human, I can contribute positively to society. I can form a nonprofit to help strengthen communities. I can bridge the gap between generations. I can connect the haves and have nots. I can develop systems to educate, inspire, and motivate the masses. I can transform millions of lives. I can lead by example. I can be the energy I want to receive. I can learn more daily. I can think clearly. I can influence positively. I can become the best version of myself.

As a servant, I will continue to do what's morally right. I will create blueprints to success. I will produce phenomenal events to bring others together. I will help educate and inform individuals on cultural differences. I will partner with software designers to create uplifting applications. I will learn multiple languages and travel around the world to share testimonies, information, and positivity. I will be righteous and upright. I will treat others with respect, kindness, and honor. I will continue to be a student of life. I will use my mind, body, and soul to make informed decisions. I will spread the light. I will become the best version of myself.

As a King, I must lead with integrity, honor, and dignity. I must establish foundations and pillars in the Kingdom. I must have peace and harmony within our Kingdom. I must keep moving forward information learned on my journey. I must connect with others so we can build collectively. I must share my missions with other like-minded, phenomenal individuals. I must educate the world and connect them to my mentors. I must stand behind words. I must understand we are one. I must learn as much as I can on this journey. I must apply knowledge, wisdom, and understand daily. I must be a creator. I must become the best version of myself.

KNOW YOUR WORTH

An edited and revised story published from Facebook

A father before he died said to his son: "Here's a crystal your grand-father gave me. But before I give it to you, go to the local jewelry stop on fourth street, and tell the representative you want to sell it, and see how much he offers to you".

He went, and then came back to his father, and said, "They offered $100 because it's had blemishes and cracks".

He replied: "Go to the pawn shop".

He went and then came back and said: "He only offered $40 father".

"Fly out to the Gemological Institution of America in Carlsbad, California".

The son thought the dad was crazy, but He went then came back, and said to his father "They offered me a million dollars for this diamond. I thought it was just a crystal".

The father said: "I wanted to let you know that the right place values you in the right way. Don't find yourself in the wrong place and get angry if you are not valued. Those that know your value are those who appreciate you, don't stay in a place where nobody sees your value".

CLOSING REMARKS

I REALIZED AN ENTREPRENEUR is not always about having the best business. It's not about making the most money. It's about finding out who you are, then adding value. It's about making a positive impact in the community. It's about discovering your hidden potentials. I had to learn how to keep faith. I had to learn how to align my mind, body and soul, with dreams, goals, and visions. I had to learn to be strong. I had to develop tough skin. I had to learn how to let go of toxic friends and habits. I had to learn how to leave toxic environments. I had to learn why my dreams mattered. I had to understand my mental health was important. I had to do research to understand who I was. I had to figure out why I wanted to be successful and define my success. I had to learn how to surrender to the will of GOD. I had to learn how to walk behind the Holy Spirit. I had to learn how to be grateful. I had to dig deeper into myself. I wanted to know thyself.

At Eric Thomas 1% event, Tiphani Montgomery emphasized the importance of making GOD the CEO of your business. I believe this is significant because GOD will direct your steps. I make motivational videos, speak, and coach others. I pray to GOD and ask him to anoint my tongue and allow me to be a vessel for him. This is my way of allowing GOD to be the CEO of those ventures. The words seem to flow like an overflowing river. I feel inspired and continue to pour whatever he pours into my heart. I wholeheartedly feel that GOD will take you from waiting on it, to walking in it. I remember waiting for the perfect moment to start this book. I remember waiting for the perfect moment to speak in front of individuals. Now, I'm a published author and public speaker. GOD is phenomenal.

Living for GOD does not mean your life is boring. Living for GOD has been the complete opposite for me. It was tough at first because of learned behaviors but once I allowed myself to surrender, miracles happened. Inside GOD's will is abundance. Everything began to flow in harmony. I gained another sense of peace and serenity. I've adapted mediation and prayer into my morning routine. I have praise breaks throughout the day. I randomly call Jesus name. I believe there's power in his name.

Every time you think you are stressed out, I want you to remember, "Stressed spelled backward is desserts." Eat every situation like it's dessert. GOD has properly equipped you. Feed your mind, body, and soul with positively charged food. Nourish your mind with knowledge so you can digest the mental food. Detox your soul from bitterness so you can taste life sweetness.

I have a vision of our old Havana Elementary School being turned into Millionaires Mindset Academy. I see professional trades, educational courses, workshops, seminars, and positive gatherings taking place there. I've seen trucking, welding, culinary, and other trade impact lives in creating positive law-abiding citizens. I've seen educational courses and workshop enriched the mindsets of families. I've seen seminars and positive events shift the trajectory of companies' businesses. We have to start using resources within our community to positively impact the communities. We must apply our knowledge, resources, and wisdom to form cooperation.

We must use our money, credit, and creativity to build. We have to stop competing and start working together.

Too many of us are victims of our environment. Let's leave the victim mindset alone. I want each one of us to learn as much as we can. Let's study as much as we can. Let's be discipline and embrace the process as much as we can. I was speaking to my brother Joel "Peewee" Andrews today. We traveled to Honolulu, Hawaii together on a business retreat with Black, Ty and other affluent, prestigious business associates. He told me he deleted his social media. He takes the time to work on his books, read books, and improve his life. He said, "One time I looked around and saw everyone looking down at their phone. I looked at the book and realized I was 60 pages ahead." Peewee has tattoos in his face. Peeweee does not wear suits everyday. However, Mr. Andrews understand the value of personal growth and self-development. He works on himself daily. He is unlocking his full potential.

I have a cousin named Gabriel Lovett, Founder of Lovetts Burger Chicken & Fries LLC, he has been working on building his business for over a year now. He has helped many college students eat quality food for an affordable price. He has provided mentorship and work opportunities for young entrepreneurs. He has graduated from Florida A & M University while running his business full time. We were delayed many times but not denied. I am confident his brand and food will be globally known. He has connected Florida State University and Florida A & M University diverse students with phenomenal food and positive energy. He's embracing the struggle of owning a fast-paced growing business. He is unlocking his full potential.

I was conversing earlier with one of my favorite teachers. She's phenomenal and I love her like a mother. She helped me understand something and I would like to share it. Every black person is not crazy. Every white person is not evil. Every black person is not a "n*gga". Every white person is not like their grandparents. There's a major cultural gap but we are still all human. Each one of us has struggles. The history is horrific. There's no way to deny it. I wrote this book as a way to help bridge the gap. I shined a positive light on our community.

I know we cannot change the gruesome history. I want us to be aware of the history. We cannot sweep it under the rug. We can't forget the history. Donald Trump said it very clearly, "You built this nation…" It could have been a political move. I'm not writing this book to stir up politics, but I am pointing out acts. We have put many years of blood, sweat, and tears into this nation. We did not inherit the benefits. However, Tyler Perry opened a studio where a Confederate army base was located. This is a phenomenal achievement. Confederated soldiers used the based to plot and plan on keeping 3.9 million Negros enslaved. Generations later, one Negro owns the land. Tyler Perry was homeless, abused, attempted suicide, and other struggles. Our community struggles are devastating. We fight through them without a therapist. We fight through them without proper guidance. All we know is fight.

We come from royal descendants, we come from leaders. Our genes are genetically geared for us to be overachievers. Melanin is valuable. Melanin is similar to having superpowers. The information available on the web, in books, and research articles back my statements. This is a phenomenal time to be alive. Let's build a nation of love, faith, and hope. Let's help everyone reach their full potential. Let's change the world. Let's create a positive nation.

Thank you for reading… Now that you have heard my story, I want you to think about yours. I want you to think about your struggles. Ask yourself, "How can I embrace my struggles to reach my full potential?" I am no different from you. I still sleep, breath, and use the restroom. All of us struggle. Rich humans struggle and poor humans struggle. Make sure you are not struggling to stay in the same position. Struggle to advance. Struggle to increase. Struggle to become the best version of yourself. Millionaires Mindset Academy is here to help you unlock your full potential. It's possible!

Made in the USA
Monee, IL
18 January 2020